THE SEDUCTION OF SOCIETY

The Seduction of Society

Pornography and Its Impact on American Life

William A. Stanmeyer

SERVANT BOOKS
Ann Arbor, Michigan

Copyright © 1984 by William A. Stanmeyer

Book design by John B. Leidy
Cover Photo by Wide World Photos

Available from Servant Publications
Box 8617, Ann Arbor, Michigan 48107

ISBN 0-89283-190-1
Printed in the United States of America

84 85 86 87 88 89 10 9 8 7 6 5 4 3 2

Library of Congress Cataloging in Publication Data

Stanmeyer, William A., 1934—
  The seduction of society.

  Bibliography: p.
  1. Pornography—United States. I. Title.
HQ471.S7 1984   363.4'7'0973   84-14097
ISBN 0-89283-190-1

Contents

To Charlie Keating
who saw the monster first,
had the courage to fight it,
and has never quit.

ONE

The Social Crisis

"SEX BUSINESS BOOMS Despite Cleanup Drive." Thus did *U.S. News and World Report* begin an article in its March 16, 1981 issue. The subhead of the essay stated:

> Adult entertainment no longer is confined to big-city porno districts. The market is moving to better neighborhoods—and even into the family home.

The writer summarized recent developments which, it is safe to say, no one could have predicted twenty-five years ago:

> Springing up now are private sex clubs, erotic boutiques and massage outcall services to add still more millions to what government sources say is at least a 4-billion-dollar annual trade.

> Even the family living room is considered fair game. There hostesses hold parties to peddle erotic paraphernalia, and home television brings X-rated movies via videotapes or cable hookups.

> Meanwhile, police, prosecutors and others who want to stop the growth of pornography and illicit sex are stymied by a patchwork of laws, constitutional roadblocks and, in many cases, lukewarm support from the public.

In 1978, *Forbes*, perhaps the most incisive of the monthly business magazines, devoted its cover story to the "four billion dollar pornography business" now booming in the United States.[1]

Virtually every American city has its "porn strip": run-down theaters with gaudy marquees hawking films showing salacious actions in zoom-lens closeup.

"Adult bookstores" are popping up not only downtown but in suburbia as well. They sell pornographic picture magazines, X-rated films, and even "sexual paraphernalia": imitation sexual organs made of rubber or plastic to use on oneself or another.

Part of the magazine rack in airports and in respectable drugstores and hotels offers a smorgasbord of sex magazines. Some will display twenty or more different publications, all featuring an apparently endless stream of nubile maidens posed seductively. Some of these magazines suggest—or even openly display—the results of sado-masochistic violence against these girls.

Many television programs, whether situation comedy or serious soap opera, constantly portray sexual pursuit and conquest—with little or no regard to marriage, family, responsibility toward children, or respect for any higher law such as God's Commandments. In many of these programs, near-nudity and off-color innuendo are main attractions; some programs would have no interest without them.

Scholarly journals in law, medicine, and public policy are giving a disturbing portrait of the pornographic subculture. For example, the 1979 issue of New York University's *Review of Law and Social Change* was titled *Violent Pornography: Degradation of Women Versus Right of Free Speech*. "Kiddie porn"—unheard of twenty years ago—now receives attention in law journals. In 1978 *Pepperdine Law Review* included an article entitled "Preying on Playgrounds: the Sexploitation of Children in Pornography and Prostitution." The summer 1980 issue of the respected Heritage Foundation journal *Policy Review* carried Dr. Ernest van den Haag's analysis of the pornophile's psychology, "Pornography and Censorship."[2] In April, 1981, the *Journal of Current Adolescent Medicine,* a journal oriented to pediatricians, provided "Extent of Pornography in Modern Society and Its Harm."

Large urban newspapers now do feature series on the pornography explosion. One such was the *Boston Globe,* which discussed

> . . .the openness with which the [pornography] industry now operates. In Los Angeles, where many adult films are made, a school recently opened to train aspiring porn stars. The Pussycat Theater chain, also in California, routinely conducts marketing surveys to gauge support for adult movies in communities where it is considering opening movie houses.[3]

The article also noted that

> A Chicago company, Bluemax Theater Channel Inc., recently announced plans to begin a hard-core film service, using a satellite to beam signals directly into homes around the country. This system. . .would be used mainly by private groups such as condominium associations.

Twenty or thirty years ago we could not have dreamed of these things happening. We can scarcely believe them today. Something dramatic has happened. What is going on?

National Morals: From Day to Night

In retrospect, it is clear that our national morals have changed considerably since World War II. Prior to 1940-45, the country as a whole adhered to the Judeo-Christian ethic of self-control. Generally speaking, our sexual relations were monogamous, our music wholesome, our films unobjectionable, our adolescent entertainments innocuous.

There was no open display of sexual materials. The calendar "pin-up" pictures of athletic girls on gas station walls were tame enough, and surely not obscene by any reasonable standard.

Whatever went on in private, public sexual morality (save perhaps among some indiscreet members of the movie industry) was uniformly straight-laced and even virtuous. Even in the mid to late 1960s, people wondered out loud whether Nelson Rockefeller, an otherwise-qualified candidate for President, would lose too many votes because of his divorce.

Departures from basic morality caused scandal, not invitations onto the talk-show circuit.

The moral tone of society was fairly high. During World War II people's energies focused on economic struggles and the national battle against the Axis powers. Immediately after the War, our national energies focused on economic expansion, building families in the suburbs, and acquiring that second car. There was a discipline in building one's assets even as, during the Depression years, there was a discipline in fighting to preserve one's assets. Whatever else they do, Depression and war and subsequent economic growth bring austerity and demand stamina, not dissipation and hedonism.

Looking back, it seems that for about fifteen to twenty years, from the end of the war till around 1960-65, society remained on a moral plateau. We built a marvelous highway network. Much of the middle class fled the cities for the sprouting suburbs. Population expanded. Incomes went up. Despite the perceived Soviet threat, people came to take domestic tranquility and material advancement for granted. Moral problems did not especially preoccupy us. If they existed in any serious way, they lay below the surface of our national public life.

Then something happened.

Whether it was Hugh Hefner and his "playboy philosophy," the explosive nihilism of the Berkeley and Columbia student riots, the troubling discovery of growing collegiate promiscuity, the scandal of so many runaway "flower children" ending up drifting, drugged, or dead, or the new "realism" in magazines and films that portrayed intimate sexual acts—

whether these were symptoms or causes or results, something happened.

Moral attitudes and public practice changed. Not all at once; and not completely. But the social consensus on moral values was shattered. Like Humpty-Dumpty in the nursery rhyme, it will take more than all the king's horses and all the king's men to put it back together again.

Public decency began to collapse. An era of violence emerged in the streets, in films, and in the all-pervasive medium of television. This violence was matched, both in the streets and in films and television, by a parallel increase of sex display, sexual innuendo, sexualized plots in fiction and sexualized crime in real life. Pornography entered American life.

The Deception of Gradual Change

It is said that if a person puts a frog into lukewarm water, and slowly heats it up toward boiling, the frog will become mesmerized, never notice the gradual increases of heat, and comfortably sit motionless while being cooked to death.

It is hard for most of us to detect gradual changes. The expansion of sexual entertainments into every medium and practically every city and town came gradually. We find it hard to compare the present with the half-forgotten 1950s and early 1960s. Only someone who has had that rare Rip-Van-Winkle experience, someone who returns to his country after years abroad, realizes the magnitude of the social change. Diplomats on overseas assignments realize it. Prisoners of war, such as the Iranian hostages absent for the relatively short span of fifteen months, realize the cultural transformation. But most of us who lived through it scarcely notice.

At some point quantitative changes add up to a change of kind. After a while, old food in the refrigerator finally spoils. After a while, constant dumping of industrial chemicals into a river pollutes the whole thing and all the fish die. After a while, too many pollutants in the air will make it harmful to breathe.

Such a change is taking place in our society because of pornography.

Years ago the word was "obscenity." Scholars wondered whether the origin of the word might lie in the playwright's sense that some forms of action—violence, blood, torture, sex—should be "off-the-scene" or offstage, better suggested than shown.

In the 1950s, when obscenity captured the attention of the Supreme Court, a group called *Citizens for Decent Literature* was formed. The question of "dirty words" in paperback novels was a key aspect of the problem. A priest, Father John Gardiner, wrote careful analyses of the degree to which books might deal with or describe erotic actions and yet be permissible in a free and virtuous society. Some of the major obscenity cases decided by the Supreme Court as late as the mid and later 1960s dealt with books.

Today it is unlikely that anyone would be prosecuted for obscene words, no matter how graphic, how depraved, how explicit. The public—and public servants such as legislators, prosecutors, judges—now tolerate what a generation ago they would have found outrageous. The water grows hotter, but the frog sits motionless.

Today the battle has shifted to visual media. Reading a novel, even one with "dirty words" in it, at least requires some effort on the part of the reader. He must actively seek out the book, block out distractions, actually read the book, and form images in his mind as he reads. But television, movies, and video cassettes require only that the viewer sit passively while the publisher or the producer gives him the images. He need only absorb them.

Pictures have replaced words. Television has replaced print as the prime mode of communication. Daily movies in the home have supplanted weekly movies at the local theatre. Today people spend upwards of forty-five hours a week watching television images on a home screen instead of a mere four hours during a weekend watching a film image on a theatre screen. Now that a spectator can actually watch what before he could only imagine, the battle over obscenity shifts ground. The change was gradual.

In short, those who wanted to limit "obscenity" had to abandon the battle against obscene words and obscene prose and instead concentrate their attention on visual pornographic acts.

And the word "pornography" has almost replaced the earlier word, "obscenity." This change is significant. For the root of the word means "whore's word" or "whore's story" or "whore's writing." These are not pleasant phrases but they are accurate, for they suggest what the films and photos make graphically explicit. The change from obscenity to pornography was gradual.

Technology did accelerate the change, however; what might have taken a couple of generations took instead only a mere decade and a half. The burgeoning "home box office" and "super TV" industries now offer "adult" or "R-rated" (often called "soft-core") films which twenty years ago would have been "X." Frequently they do offer "X-rated" films. Many hotels and motels have video-cable hookups which permit their guests to watch such films for a few dollars. So instead of having to go downtown to the porn theaters in "combat zone" neighborhoods, the discreet voyeur can sit back in the comfort of his own room to indulge his fantasies. More people are doing this not only because it is easier, but because it seems socially approved—like watching Monday night football.

This change is recent, yet we scarcely notice. The water begins to steam, but the frog sits motionless.

Our movies have changed enormously in less than twenty years. A film such as *Deep Throat*, described in the court opinion quoted immediately below, could not have been marketed around the country in the 1950s or early 1960s. Judge Joel Tyler, one of the few judges around the country to uncompromisingly condemn this film, described it this way:

. . .The film runs 62 minutes. It is in color and in sound, and boasts a musical score. Following the first innocuous scene. . .the film runs from one act of explicit sex into another, forthrightly demonstrating heterosexual intercourse and a variety of deviated sexual acts. . . . The camera angle, emphasis and closeup zooms were directed. . ."toward a maximum exposure in detail of the genitalia" during the gymnastics, gyrations, bobbing, trundling, surging, ebb and flowing, eddying, moaning, groaning and sighing, all with ebullience and gusto.

There were so many and varied forms of sexual activity one would tend to lose count of them. . . .Nothing was faked or simulated, it was as explicit and exquisite as life. . . .

The defense experts testified that they see the film legitimatizing woman's need and "life right" (as one put it) for sexual gratification, equal with that of men. They also see in the film the thoughtful lesson that sex should not be unavailingly monolithic. . .but should take varied forms. . . .These unusual and startling revelations are of social value, they say, not only for the bedroom, but necessary as an object lesson for a public forum. . . .

The alleged story lines are a facade, the sheer negligee through which clearly shines the producer's and the defendant's true and only purpose; that is, the presentation of unmistakably hard-core pornography. . . .

"Deep Throat"—a nadir of decadence—is indisputably obscene by any legal measurement. . . .

Its dominant theme, and in fact, its only theme is to appeal to prurience in sex. It is hard-core pornography with a vengeance. "It creates an abstract paradise in which the only emotion is lust and the only event orgasm and the only inhabitants animated phalluses and vulvae" (Anthony Burgess, speaking of pornography generally, and well applied here). . . . Justice Stewart says he knows hard-core pornography when he merely sees it. . .We have seen it in "Deep Throat" and this is one throat that deserves to be cut. I readily perform the operation in finding the defendant guilty as charged.[4]

The Modern Fagins of Lust

Today we have a type of pornography that is a category all by itself. It was utterly unknown two decades ago. This is child pornography, often called—without hinting adequately its evil—"kiddie porn."

This is the use of minor children, sometimes as young as toddlers scarcely able to walk, in pornographic pictures and films. Most of these children, normally under the age of fourteen, are boys and girls who drift through our big cities, looking for a thrill or simply fleeing an unhappy home. They have no marketable skills. They are too young to work—legally. They soon fall prey to the Fagins of our time, who promise some food, a bit of affection, a place to sleep, protection from the unknown horrors of the darkness—all in return for "acting" in a film the promisor wants to shoot. Other motivations are the attraction of drugs or fear of threats.

Whatever the reason, thousands of pre-adolescent and adolescent youngsters get drawn into the pornography-prostitution-narcotics subculture. For them, this subculture provides a life based on exploitation of others, self-hatred, high risks, venereal disease, and rapid obsolescence. Most are "burnt out" by the time they are twenty.

In 1977 at least 264 different magazines sold in "adult bookstores" that dealt with sexual acts between children or between children and adults. The average price of these magazines was over $7.00. In 1976 Los Angeles police estimated that adults sexually exploited over 30,000 children that year. In 1975, Houston police found a warehouse full of pornography, including 15,000 slides of boys in homosexual acts, over 1,000 magazines and paperbooks, plus a thousand reels of film. In New York City, Father Bruce Ritter, a Franciscan priest who started Covenant House, a group of shelters for runaway children, reported that "Of the 12,000 kids under 21 who come to. . .Covenant House for help, fully 60 percent have been involved in prostitution or pornography."[5] Some of them are visual fodder in such magazines as *Lollitots*, which shows girls eight to fourteen and *Moppits* showing children aged three to twelve, and playing cards that picture naked, spread-eagled children.[6]

One New York distributor of "chicken films"—the vernacular for pornographic films involving children—advertises ten films in its "lollypops" series. The ads show cartoons of two nude, very young boys licking lollypops, the slogan "Chicken Films come of Age," and graphic descriptions of sex acts, including "Ronnie, Bobby and Eddie—three preteens on a bed." The movies are 8mm, in color, 200 feet, and $20.00 each. There is an address, but the telephone directory assistance has no phone listed. Though police undercover agents arrested the firm's owner and charged him with promoting obscenity, the district attorney explained that under criminal statutes then in force, the police cannot confiscate the films. All they could do is charge him with a misdemeanor. The D.A. added that "We still don't know who the children are or where they come from."

Other magazine titles include: *Nudist Moppets, Chicken Delight, Naughty Horny Imps, Chicken Love,* and *Child Discipline.* In searching the house of a man suspected of molesting children in Michigan a few years ago, police came across a collection of hundreds of such magazines, all illustrated in bright color with close-ups stressing fair skin and genitals. Robin Lloyd, author of the book *For Money or Love: Boy Prostitution in America,* documented the involvement of 300,000 boys, aged eight to sixteen, in the pornography/prostitution rackets. Dr. Judianne Densen-Gerber, whose efforts helped persuade Congress in 1977 to pass the first Sexual Exploitation of Minors Act, noted that Lloyd spoke only of boys, a fact, she stated, that "leads me to believe that if there are 300,000 boys, there must be a like number of girls, but no one has bothered to count them."[7] She added:

Lloyd postulated but cannot substantiate that only half the true number of these children is known. That would put the figure closer to 1,200,000 nationwide—a figure that is not improbable to me. . .How many ways are there for a twelve-year-old to support himself or herself?

The answer is, a child can support himself or herself—for a time—by turning one's life over to our modern Fagins.

Is There a "Crisis"?

Many observers doubt that the spread of pornography has really caused a crisis. They note that urban life always had its raw side, that abuse of homeless children was prevalent as long ago, say, as Charles Dickens' time. They argue that pornography causes no lasting harm, that after awhile people will get bored with it, that permissive Sweden and Denmark have not sunk into the sea.

Many law professors declare that pornography is a necessary price we must pay for freedom of speech. Sociologists say that what has changed is not so much the quantity and quality of modern pornography as our attentiveness to it. Libertarian social philosophers say that "People will do it anyway," and that "It is not the law's business" to tell people what to read.[8]

Observers like these are saying that there is no crisis, even if not all of their propositions address the question of whether there is a "crisis." Insofar as they think nothing can or should be done about pornography, to that extent they say that it *does not matter* whether there really is a crisis.

The decision to try to "do something about it" depends on how serious the "it" is. One reacts differently to heartburn than to a heart attack; one remains calm or becomes excited, depending on whether he is viewing a banked campfire spitting out a few errant sparks, or a raging forest fire engulfing acres of timber.

This much the reader surely will grant: that in the root sense of the word *crisis*—from a Greek word meaning, literally, a *decision*—we have come to a turning point, a decisive or critical moment. Either the law and courts and the public as a whole will "draw a line somewhere" to stop at least the more extreme forms of pornography (such as sadomasochism or sexual exploitation of minors) or the use of certain modes of communication (such as cable TV and cassettes for the home) or they will draw no line at all. The nation will decide that certain kinds of sexual actions and displays will not be permitted for commercial gain—or it will permit everything in every place. Either "anything goes" or "some things will be prohibited." The choice is not between total permissiveness and total repression; it is between total permissiveness and repression of some erotic depictions in some places.

To provide the basis for a reasoned judgment, the next chapter will explore more precisely the answer to the question, "What is pornography?"

TWO

What Pornography Is

"THIS IS A TELEVISION STATION in Chicago [naming the station] calling. Can you come up here tomorrow for the taping of a four-man talk show debate on obscenity? We want to have two people on each side, and we understand you are qualified to take the anti-obscenity position." Thus began an unexpected call I received at Indiana University Law School in February of 1977.

"Who else will be your guests?" I asked.

"On your side, Bill Berg, who runs his own talk show on another station, WGN Radio. On the other side, Harry Reems and Larry Flynt. Reems played in 'Deep Throat.' Flynt publishes *Hustler* magazine."

I asked how they got my name and why me, since there are six law schools in Chicago, two of which are church-affiliated. I thought there should be at least one local law professor who would be willing to debate Mr. Flynt on television. The answer was that no one else whom they had called wanted to do it.

Fearful that the argument would go to the other side by default, I accepted, with one condition: "Berg and I may not be the attraction for your audience, but if you want a day of my professional time for no stipend, you owe me one concession: we get equal time." Without hesitation, the television producer agreed.

As it turned out, however, they broke that promise. Reems

and Flynt were allowed to argue their case to a sympathetic moderator and audience for eighteen minutes before Bill Berg and I were invited to come on camera. But the occasion provided me the unwelcome opportunity to glance through *Hustler* magazine just before the show, courtesy of the program producer.

It contained photo close-ups of sexual organs in sex acts, ads for child-like dolls that simulated sex acts, interviews with prostitutes, a "cartoon" laughing at child abuse ("Chester the Molester"), and other pictures too debased to mention. My momentary brush with this filth did help in a surprising way during the program.

Mr. Flynt insisted at one point that "You wouldn't want to censor a discussion of sex like this program. Then why do you want to censor *Hustler?*" To which I responded "If *Hustler* magazine is merely a 'discussion of sex,' like a gynecology text, then let the cameraman focus back there where the producer has a copy; zoom in on the pictures that *Hustler* contains, and give the people of Chicago a close-up. Let *them* decide whether *Hustler* is just a medical text."

The reaction to this brazen challenge was consternation in, the glass-walled control booth: hands signaling, "No, No, Don't!'": grimaces conjuring up angry F.C.C. lawyers; faces anticipating angry phone calls from the audience.

So we kept debating the merits of *Hustler* without the audience knowing what was in it, and arguing the merits of censorship without anyone knowing what we were censoring.

Ironically, we were censoring not pornography—but the public's knowledge of what pornography is. For want of a better term, I call this communications vacuum about pornography "reverse censorship."

The Reasons for Reverse Censorship

There are learned law review articles, indeed whole collections of them,[1] in which most of the writers spend thousands of words on abstractions like freedom of speech but are silent about the concrete images—pornographic pictures and words—to which their abstractions are meant to apply.

There are debaters in many public forums, such as the ubiquitous "civil liberties" attorneys, who expound on talk shows and in legislative hearings about the evils of trying to control pornography—but never give their listeners examples of the "anything" which, at root, they say "goes."

There are many legal briefs filed with appellate courts asking the judges to overthrow obscenity convictions—but few if any of these briefs include appendices with photos or detailed verbal descriptions of what obscenities are at stake in the case.

There are good reasons for this informal censorship. The "civil liberties" attorneys know their cause would suffer a severe setback if the public, the juries, and the judges were to pull the mask off the face of pornography and see how hideous it really is.

The point came home to me in a trial in Virginia which I sat in on a few years ago. The managers of a notorious "adult book store" were tried on eleven felony counts of violating the state's anti-pornography laws by marketing pornographic films. They pled guilty to five of the counts before the trial so that the jury would not have to view the films involved—scenes of sex with animals, sadomasochism, and sex with children—and be so outraged that their anger would spill over onto the other six films and motivate a conviction there too. (The other six were depictions of normal intercourse, scenes presumably less offensive to the jury's sense of community morals.)

There is another reason why television, general-circulation newspapers and magazines, and other communications media do not tell the public what pornography is. They are constrained by the canons of good taste, or at least by anticipated public reaction which might harm their circulation or advertising revenue. To their credit, newspapers hesitate to dignify pornographic pulp novels by reprinting lurid passages. Neither do they want to lower the tone of their Sunday supplements by reprinting the contents of *Hustler*.[2] There are standards of decent communication. Giving people first-hand experience of what pornography is will violate those standards in a newspaper or television program of general audience interest.

The distinguished liberal political scientist Reo M. Christenson stated the problem this way:

> Those appalled by the prospect of censorship usually do not realize what they are protecting, or what, through postal subsidies, they help distribute with their tax dollars.
>
> It is imperative that the public know what is really in *Hustler*. . .[It] is not a 'girlie' magazine or another *Playboy*. Rather, it is full of pictures and descriptions of such gross sexual perversion, such bizarre forms of bestiality and such nauseating accounts of excretory activities that few if any newspapers feel free to explicitly inform their reader of what is in the magazine.[3]

The same problem befalls the speaker. If he stands before a mixed audience, and especially if any part of that audience is unfamiliar with the genre, and most particularly if any of the audience should be young people—then he simply cannot go into detail. To do so distracts and offends: some of the hearers think he is indulging in the same contrived titillation he condemns. Everyone will feel dirtied by the encounter with real pornography.

So the paradox is that the promoters of pornography are freer than their opponents. They can distribute obscenity more freely than critics can distribute information about what they are doing.

The Need for Candor

Without a "gut reaction" to a practice abstractly viewed as evil, people will not do anything about it. Very few people are moved by abstract principles. The general need for "virtue" as a foundation for a democratic republic, however true as a matter of accurate political theory, will bring about no more action than a yawn. Indeed, the importance of seat belts to safe driving does not "come home to" us through recitation of Labor Day weekend statistics about highway deaths. Being in or seeing an auto accident where failure to use the seat belt caused death *will* motivate a man to buckle up the next time.

Pornography works on the imagination. To assess how seriously pornography might change a person's imagination and consequent moral perceptions, it is necessary to have clearly in mind—simply as a clinical datum—the nature, the range, the variety, and the intensity of pornographic images.

Assume that an advertising agency is trying to persuade a potential client, a company which brews "lite" beer, to engage the agency to create its television commercials. The agency would do more than provide statistics about how its commercials increased other clients' sales. The agency would also show actual videotaped commercials which its creative department had concocted. To let the client see their work is much more effective than simply to give him numbers and words about it. The saying attributed to Confucius, "one picture worth 10,000 words," is true. Advertising relies on it. So must an effort to inform people about what pornography is.

We will not show pictures in this book. But I am going to describe some pornography. I do so reluctantly, only because it is necessary.

In 1957, Charles H. Keating, Jr., an attorney in Cincinnati, became concerned about the spread of obscenity. He founded a citizens' group later called *Citizens for Decency through Law*, which still is active and today is one of the three leading organizations in the country giving ordinary citizens a vehicle through which they can multiply and focus their efforts in the fight to preserve public morality.[4] The publisher of this book asked Mr. Keating how specific this writer should become in detailing examples of pornography. He responded:

> . . . I reluctantly agree that it is absolutely necessary to give concrete examples of pornography. Specifically [such lurid examples as the publisher had provided him comprised material which] is called for.
>
> When I first began the fight against pornography the question you pose troubled me seriously. I asked Archbishop Karl Alter of Cincinnati (since deceased) for advice. He agreed that in order to present the problem it was necessary to graphically depict it. Otherwise the audience would not understand. Considering the flood tide of filth engulfing America there is hardly reason to think that a presentation like [the one you plan to publish] could have anything but a good effect.
>
> I pointed out [recently] that the principal reason the cancer of pornography was not curbed lay in the fact that decent people rightly revolt and are repulsed by the idea of working with it, even in the combat against it.[5]

Examples of Pornography

In this section I will summarize some illustrations of pornography and provide, in a few cases, enough verbal description that the reader might grasp the essence of the pornographic image involved. As prior sections have made clear, my purpose is neither to titillate nor to offend. If the ordinary reader will forgive what may strike him as rather gross, he can focus his energies on understanding, analysis, and reflection. He should remember too that what may not move him because it is only verbally described could well capture his imagination and excite his passions if depicted in living color and revealing close-up.

Exploitation Film. Professor Harry Clor describes a typical movie showing in one of the many New York exploitation film theaters just off Times Square:

> In *The Morbid Snatch* two men conceive and execute a plan to capture a young girl, imprison her, and compel her to submit to sexual acts of various sorts. The girl is drugged, confined in a basement, stripped naked, and subjected to sexual intercourse, first with one of the men, then with a lesbian, and then with both the man and the lesbian simultaneously. Periodically, the camera focuses very closely upon the sexual organs of all participants. Periodically also the girl (whose age is, perhaps by intention, difficult to determine; she could be as young as sixteen or as old as twenty-five) is represented as responding erotically to these acts. The sexual scenes, and preparation for them, constitute practically the sole content and surely the sole interest of this film. A companion film about twenty minutes long consists of nothing but close-up shots of a nude woman masturbating. The 'coming attactions' promise films devoted to rape, violence, mass orgies, and the intercourse of women with apes.[6]

Magazine Photos Dehumanizing Women. In reporting on a slide lecture developed by a new feminist anti-pornography group, Women Against Violence Against Women, Sarah J. McCarthy states:

> The slide show includes a *Hustler* cover picture of a nude woman being pushed head first into a meat grinder, coming out at the bottom as ground meat. . . . Inside this issue is a nude woman lying on a plate looking like a piece of chicken covered with ketchup, and another who is laid out on a hamburger bun, also covered with ketchup. Another issue of *Hustler*. . .has a drawing of a man's scrotum pushed up against the ear of a retarded girl, his

penis presumably filling up her empty head and semen squirting out the other ear. The text reads ''Good Sex with Retarded Girls. . . .''

The rest of the slide show is more of the same. Women hanging on crosses, their nipples being pulled with pliers, and a kiddie porn section that assures anyone with child abuse on his mind that it's okay, the kids will love it. 'I never dreamed it would be this wonderful,' said one nude little girl in saddle shoes; and a little girl in a *Playboy* cartoon, getting dressed as she leaves the apartment of a sixty-year-old man, says, 'and you call *that* being molested?'[7]

This same slide lecture provided the content of an article by Theresa Hommel, ''Images of Women in Pornography,'' the transcript of which includes these comments:

The next slide is extremely violent, so be prepared. This is from *Chic Magazine*, published by Larry Flynt productions. . . .The title is *Columbine Cuts Up.* The images show a woman stabbing herself in the vagina with a large butcher knife, and in the other two pictures, cutting her labia and breasts with a scissors. The picture is horrible, but take a minute to contemplate what is happening and why. In such pornography the camera action is done 'first person.' You might see a pair of male hands enter the scene from the front and torture or tie up a woman, but you never see the actual man himself. Thus, men can remain anonymous and victimize women without taking responsibility for the crime.[8]

Live Pornographic Entertainment. As long ago as 1970, there was at least one ''club'' in New York whose patrons came for the sake of entertaining themselves by watching sexual performances. As described in the high quality public affairs journal, *The Public Interest*, Club Orgy offered group voyeurism:

At Club Orgy, Rita and Victor perform sexual intercourse twice daily to a grim but attentive audience. . . [They] are still the Fonteyn and Nureyev of public sex, at least at Club O. The stage of the theatre is occupied by a large bed, which Victor thoughtfully makes before each show. The lights come up on Rita, negligeed, reading some porn, and cooing for her husband, Victor returns home from work—'it's not just intercourse,' he explained, 'we have a lot of lines'—and the two begin 20 minutes of inventive and gymnastic sex. . . The show ends a bit abruptly when all the theatre lights start flashing, and Rita and Victor uncouple like an electric train. . . .[9]

Adult Bookstores.   There are 15,000 to 20,000 adult bookstores in the United States, and even those in the sparsely populated areas, have monthly gross receipts ranging from $10,000 to $18,000 each.[10] Books are not the only items sold. Rather, most of the "bookstores" also feature peep shows where, for a quarter, a patron can watch two or three minutes of a hard-core film. Besides the wide variety of printed material, sectionalized according to sexual preference, these stores usually sell sex novels, 8mm and 16mm hard-core films, and pre-recorded video cassettes.

But what makes many of these stores unique, and warrants noting them in this section, is the open display of "sexual devices" or "sexual paraphernalia." These include plastic/rubber penises which are usually hung, by the dozens, from shelves at eye level.

Thus the visitor enters a fantasy world where shame, decency, privacy, or the sacred have no place; where sex acts are the sole interest and where a person can, for reasons that elude anyone who is normal, purchase artificial sex organs for self-entertainment. Because the sex marketing in these stores in so blatant and obtrusive, just to walk through one is a pornographic experience.

X-Rated Mix of Sex and Violence in Films. The scenario next summarized, part of *Super Vixens,* a nearly obscene film making the rounds of movie theaters in the mid-1970s, itself may not be pornographic under the Supreme Court's current standards. The Court declines to admit that sadistic violence and sexual pornography have a common denominator: the dehumanization of the victim in a way that draws the audience, in imagination, into the dehumanizing action, which is depicted as enjoyable. Still, it deserves inclusion here, as an example of the Saturday-night entertainment typically available to eighteen-year-olds in every major city:

> A muscular and sadistically-inclined off-duty cop, taunted by his voluptuous one-night paramour because he cannot achieve erection despite her intense stimulation, hacks apart and breaks down the door to the bathroom where, scarcely clothed, she has begun to comb her hair preparatory to bathing; in a rage he beats, stomps, and hacks her into a bloody pulp and finishes the slaughter by tossing a live electric heater into the crimson tub water in which she lies moaning. This act apparently electrocutes his tortured half-conscious victim. Well spiced with leers, shouts, and screams, the torment and agony of a woman beautiful only moments before takes place up close, in livid color, and precise detail. The perpetrator of this barbarity caps off his crime by burning her house down, the audience unsure whether despite her wounds she might still be alive. In this bizarre nightmare fantasy, shown of course on the usual wide movie screen filling one's whole field of vision, the killer copy goes unpunished and, miraculously, the victim reappears shortly later, unscathed, playing a different character having the same oversexed qualities.

Films and Photos of Explicit Sex by Children. A growing field of pornography or near-pornography is the practice of depicting children in seductive poses or actual sex acts. The ordinary citizen may be both quite puzzled and shocked that there should be a market for films of young boys masturbating, for instance, but the following statement from the *Petition for a Writ of Certiorari* by the District Attorney of New York should demonstrate that someone spent the time to find cooperative subjects, film the action, duplicate the prints, and distribute them to marketing centers.

> On March 2, 1981, Paul Ira Ferber, the owner of a Manhattan bookstore specializing in pornography, sold two films to an undercover police officer. The films are devoted almost exclusively to depicting young boys masturbating. The first film shows a naked young boy lying face down on a bed, rubbing against the bed. After a while, the boy turns over onto his back and masturbates twice to ejaculation. Then, lying on his side, he places a dildo between his buttocks as if to insert it into his anus. The second film includes scenes of other naked boys, including some no older than seven or eight years of age, jumping, sitting, and reclining on a mattress. In addition, these boys are engaged in solo and mutual masturbation and in conduct suggesting oral-genital contact. At the end of the second film, the main child performer dresses very slowly, then picks up what appears to be United States currency and holds it toward the camera.[11]

How-To-Do-It Rape Manuals. Quite a bit of pornography caters to male aggression. In many cases the male actor is only suggested, as, for example, where only his hands appear; or where his facial features are hidden: this photographic device enables the viewer more easily to "step into the shoes" of the anonymous perpetrator, and it gives an Everybody's-doing-it suggestion. (The anonymous man is Everyman.) Thus one well-known pornographic magazine featured, some years ago, a "step-by-step" exposition, with detailed color photos, of the techniques of rape. It highlighted the range of possibilities for the rapist if he would tie the girl down.

On one occasion the Michigan State Police apprehended a rapist in the very act: he had the woman tied down and had the magazine propped up nearby, opened to the how-to-do-it pictures.

Though this actual case was probably unknown to Law Professor Tom Gerety, one may assume that the frequency of rape depiction in pornography motivated him to compose two hypothetical examples of the genre for the sake of legal/aesthetic analysis:

> First, a film produced outside the United States but now showing in a discrete (sic) downtown theater. Call it *In Every Infant's Cry of Fear*. It depicts a band of grown men who kidnap, molest, rape, and finally dismember small children of four or five. All of this in great and sober detail, a sexual ritual in which the camera focuses on the physiological excitations which accompany the violent uses of these children's bodies.

> Secondly, a regional magazine called *Sex Now*, sold in a plain brown wrapper from behind the counter of a local tobacco shop. This month it features a clinically and suggestively illustrated article entitled, "The Joy of Rape: How To, Why To, Where To." It carries an appendix of local maps together with notes on "How To Get Away With It."[12]

Besides the foregoing illustration, other forms of pornography include zoom-lens close-ups of: women having intercourse with dogs and horses. . .lesbian masturbation and the devices enabling lesbian copulation. . .homosexual sadomasochism, with instruments, . . .fetishistic ways to stimulate oneself autoerotically, e.g., demonstrations of how to hang oneself by a woman's undergarments, long enough to become aroused. . .and even "snuff films" in which the victim is attacked sexually and then *actually murdered before the camera.*[13]

These examples of pornography are crude, offensive, and even barbaric. Yet, repulsive as these descriptions are, they scarcely capture the enormity of the impact of pornography on American culture as a whole. There are not just a few prints of these photos; there are thousands of prints. There are not just one or two films showing these actions; there are thousands of them. The young man—and it is usually a man, though they are not always young—who entertains himself with such material as I have described is not limited to a few opportunities. He can find hundreds of pictures, hundreds of films, and very soon he will be able to find hundreds of videocassettes. It is possible to spend hours and hours and hours watching or reading pornographic depictions; it is now possible—and for some younger people this has happened—for a man's main entertainment to consist of watching other people engage in various forms of ultimate sexual activity.

How can this glut of pornography not affect behavior? Incredibly, there is debate about this question. Let us see what we know about it.

THREE

Pornography and Behavior

A T ONE TIME IT WAS FASHIONABLE to call pornography a "victimless" crime. This is said to be a crime which "harms no one" except, perhaps, the perpetrator—an action which has a high degree of moral content but is deemed to do little or no civic damage. In the eyes of those who would "decriminalize" victimless crimes, pornography is a private vice like alcoholism and gambling and, some would say, narcotics addiction. It is, or should be, no concern of the law because it allegedly does no harm. Supposedly, no anti-social behavior follows from involvement with pornography. "No girl was ever corrupted by a book."

The view that pornography causes no harm—not even neurosis or medical harm such as venereal disease due to increased sexual experimentation—is a generalized expression of the view that "pornography does not cause crime." The majority of the members of the Presidential Commission on Obscenity and Pornography subscribed to this position. They based their decision that pornography does not adversely affect behavior on responses to questionnaires sent to numerous psychiatrists and clinical psychologists, and from the inconclusive results of studying the physical reactions of college students who volunteered to experiment with viewing pornography.[1]

Twelve of the eighteen Commissioners concurred in the finding that:

> Empirical research designed to clarify the question has found no evidence to date that exposure to explicit sexual materials plays a significant role in the causation of delinquent or criminal behavior among youth or adults (p. 32), or causes "social or individual harms such as crime, delinquency, sexual or non-sexual deviancy or severe emotional disturbance." (p. 58).[2]

Two of the Commission members, Morris Lipton and Edward Greenwood, somewhat incautiously asserted with apodictic certainty that pornography causes no harm. They took this position with such vehemence that they issued this strong statement.

> We would have welcomed evidence relating exposure to erotica to delinquency, crime and anti-social behavior, for if such evidence existed we might have a simple solution to some of our most urgent problems. However, the work of the commission has failed to uncover such evidence. They [the research studies] fail to establish a meaningful causal relationship or *even significant correlation* [emphasis added] between exposure to erotica and immediate or delayed antisocial behavior among adults. To assert the contrary from available evidence is not only to deny the facts, but also to delude the public. . .(p. 452)

This "no-harm" statement, which contradicts some of the findings of the Commission's own technical researchers, was soon challenged by other social scientists also possessing impressive credentials.[3] But its propagandistic influence perdures: popular articles and even learned journals continue to assert that the Commission "found" that pornography causes no harm whatsoever, despite the immediate dissents of the Commission minority.

The Connection with Sex Crimes

The dissenters to that view, layman Charles H. Keating, Jr., Father Morton A. Hill, S.J., and Methodist minister Winfrey Link, did see a connection between pornography and "harm" in the evidence they assembled. The U.S. Senate, in voting 60-5 to reject the majority report of the commission, clearly sided with the dissenters. They all were saying in effect, that sometimes a girl *is* corrupted by a man who has read a book— and got the idea from that book. Some criminal cases in the 1970s indicate a measure of truth to their view. Thus, in one 1973 case:

A 35-year-old man on trial for kidnapping told, on the witness stand, how he developed a compulsion to act out the bizarre photos in pornographic magazines he purchases at local adult book stores. He used a knife to force a girl into his car, because, he said, "I had the burning desire to carry through what I had read in those books." When arrested, two boxes containing 177 pornographic books were found in his car.[4]

In another case, which reached a State Supreme Court, the defendant admitted at trial that he watched two little girls, age eight and ten, near their school for some time; he further admitted that he frequented adult bookstores and at the time was reading a pornographic book and that one of the little girls reminded him of the girl in his book. He kidnapped them, sexually abused both, and killed one.[5]

Michigan authorities used a computer to analyze thousands of sex-related crimes committed over two decades in that state. Detective Lieutenant Darrell Pope, a Vice Investigator with the State Police, in a public lecture on May 1, 1979, titled, "Does

Pornographic Literature Incite Sexual Assaults?'' gave numerous cases where the assailants had immersed themselves in pornographic films or pictures and then gone out and committed sex crimes. These crimes included rape, sodomy, and even the bizarre erotic crime of piquerism (piercing with a knife till blood flows, a kind of sexual torture). In some cases the attacker admitted that the urge to rape or torture erotically came over him while reading an obscene picture magazine or attending a movie showing rape and erotic torture.

In 1969 during the early months of the Presidential Commission on Obscenity and Pornography, Charles H. Keating, Jr., whose civic efforts had been instrumental in motivating Congress to establish this very investigative body, wrote to William B. Lockhart, chairman, to complain that the Commission's methodology was flawed:

> . . .I note that, in the area of antisocial behavior, there is an abundance of projected studies by social scientists into the theoretical aspects of antisocial behavior, but little, if any, time, money or study is being devoted to the practical aspect of what has actually been happening.[6]

Keating went on to urge a careful statistical study of the relationship between pornography and sex crimes. Rather than questionnaires directed to psychologists, he requested the Commission to authorize a review of real-life case histories, as documented from police files and investigator experience. He recommended searching for ''type'' situations, ''using actual examples acquired from various sources over the past few years.'' Keating provided twenty-six documented cases then fairly recent; some of these are listed below:

> *Murder-Sexual Perversion.* Male, age 27, and female, age 23, murder a girl, aged 10, and boys, ages 12 and 17. Prior to their death, murderers employed torture and sexual perversion and tape recorded the events. Lewd photographs of young girls in pornographic poses and a

library of pornographic and sadistic literature (DeSade) were found in the male's possession.

Rape Case. Seven Oklahoma teenage male youths gang attack a 15-year-old female from Texas, raping her and forcing her to commit unnatural acts with them. Four of the youths, two the sons of attorneys, admit being incited to commit the act by reading obscene magazines and looking at lewd photographs.

Assault. Male youth, age 13, admits attack on a young girl in a downtown office was stimulated by sexual arousal from a stag magazine article he had previously read in a public drugstore, which showed naked women and an article on "How to Strip a Woman."

Attempted Rape. A 15-year-old boy stabbed a 9-year-old girl, dragged her into the brush and was ripping off her clothes. The girl screamed and the youth fled. The next day he was picked up by police. He admitted that he had done the same thing [in two other cities]. He said that his father kept pornographic pictures in his top dresser drawer and that each time he pored over them the urge would come over him.

Rape Case. Santa Clara County District Attorney Louis Bergna reports, as printed in San Jose, Calif., *Mercury,* Nov. 23, 1966:

Santa Clara County crime file documents cases where teenage boys have attacked, and killed, women after their sex drives were ignited by lewd photos from readily available men's magazines. One youth after seeing a beautiful young girl kidnapped and held prisoner in the British movie, *The Collector,* carted off a girl and held her for 18 hours while he forced her to commit every act you can possibly imagine. In his home we found nothing but this type of magazine.

Juvenile Delinquency-Child Molestation. A male individual brings 2 girls, age 13 and 15, into his home which is filled with obscene literature and has relations with them.

Needless to say, these examples demonstrate a *correlation* between pornographic indulgence and criminal behavior. By themselves, they do not prove pornography *causes* sex crimes, although the distinction between correlation and causality is often almost impossible to make in practice. It may well be that some people with a pre-existing propensity toward sex crimes such as rape and child molestation are drawn to pornography because of this inclination. However, we cannot dismiss the clear evidence of some causality, especially in those cases where the perpetrator himself confesses he felt "compelled" to act out his fantasy after first looking at the porn.

Amoral Attitudes and Immoral Actions

In a book highly critical of modern psychology and its "selfist" assumptions, Paul C. Vitz, the distinguished New York University professor of psychology, noted that the pursuit of pleasure necessarily requires ever-increasing stimuli just to maintain the same level of enjoyment:

That in satisfying our biological hungers *we often devour ourselves and others* receives little or no emphasis from self-theorists, despite the well-documented psychological principle that the *adaptation level for pleasure* (or the level for optimum stimulation by our environment) *constantly moves up* with experience. This "relativity of pleasure" pushes people to more and more extreme situations just to keep the amount of pleasure constant. In practice, this leads to diminishing pleasure, because of the increasingly negative side-effects of the more extreme conditions.[7]

Professor Vitz uses this insight to explain, in part, marital discontent due to the "cognitive dissonance" between unrealistic expectations and inadequate experiences. Yet it also surely helps explain both the causal factor in the correlation between pornography and sex crimes and something of the evolution of pornography toward ever more violent and degrading forms in the last twenty years.

Does pornography affect behavior? We must keep in mind what pornography is: the visual depiction of ultimate erotic acts, such as sexual intercourse, portrayed in such a way as to stimulate the psychology and imagination of the viewer. The viewer vicariously engages in the same sex acts and experiences, through masturbatory fantasy, intense sexual pleasure. Pornography is thus far different from art, which does not seek to immerse the viewer in the depiction in order to stimulate him erotically.[8] One crosses the not-so-fine line from art to erotica when the depiction becomes overwhelmingly sexual, ultimate and active, with zoom-lense close-ups of sexual acts and sexual organs, and with proportionate loss of attention, meaning, or respect for the person sexually used. This person becomes no more than a function of an organ: a momentary source of pleasure for the viewer. One also crosses the line when the depiction glorifies unnatural sexual activity, such as men with prepubescent boys or women with animals.

As Professor Vitz points out, the adaptation level for pleasure constantly moves up with experience. Simply, it takes more to get less. A person must use ever more extreme forms of pornographic incitement to obtain the same level of arousal and consequent pleasure. Since pornography teaches that what it shows is enjoyable, the practitioner of imaginative masturbation suspects that really *doing it* would be even more enjoyable. As watching begins to cloy, the need for ''optimum stimulation'' moves him to try it.

Indeed, we have seen such a progression in the evolution of pornographic forms over the last two decades. The practice of pornographic depiction, whether films or photos, has changed drastically over a short period. As recently as 1960 it primarily depicted normal heterosexual intercourse between adults. As the clientele became rapidly sated, the need for new stimuli drove the producers of pornography into an endless quest for new titillations. Thus during the past twenty years they have turned to using young people of both sexes, teen and preteen, and to depicting practices long considered unnatural, such as sodomy and sadomasochism. In seeking ways to intensify the autoerotic sexual experience, pornographers resemble drug pushers seeking to hold their market by offering greater "highs" through purer heroin and larger doses of cocaine.

Does pornography affect behavior? The user of pornography must divorce himself entirely from all inhibitions, sense of modesty, and feelings of shame about watching other people perform sexual acts. He must deny the cultural assumptions that condemn the voyeurism he indulges. He must reject any feelings of guilt by allowing himself to become absorbed into the pornographic experience. Of course, one's *own* erotic activity is more absorbing than merely being a spectator of *other* men's erotic activity. Thus there is a strong temptation to move from being viewer to being actor, from spectator to participant.

This transition is easy for the pornophile because pornography has freed him from inhibitions. By indulging his profane curiosities to the limit—by entertaining himself by watching, and vicariously re-enacting in imagination, such acts as pedophilia and sado-masochism and bestiality—he radically severs his own new amorality from the cultural norms which continue to hold these actions and his voyeurism about them to be perverse. The pornophile is freed from the "straight" world—and its values which urge respect for humans and some measure of self-control in sexual activity. He is ready to do the things he has already approved others doing.

Pornography does not "cause" crime every time a man immerses his mind in it, but pornography does certainly cause a change in attitude. It may not always "cause" crime in the sense that Isaac Newton noted physical causality: one billiard ball strikes another and causes that second ball to fall into the pocket. But it is a mistake to think that all evils which befall a society or an individual are direct, immediate, and physical. Pornography is so often associated with sex crimes because it is "predispositive cause": it creates an attitude in which crime is easier to commit. Thus it indirectly affects behavior.

A Predisposition to Crime

We commonly recognize "predispositive" causes of anti-social conduct in other areas. For example, it is widely believed that poverty "causes" crime in the sense that poor people are predisposed to anti-social conduct, even though it happens frequently enough that poor people are more honest than rich people. As Harry Clor has observed:

> We do not find that all, or most, poor people become criminals or that all criminals are poor people, yet poverty is regarded as a cause of crime, though the cause-and-effect relationship can be proved to be operative in only a small minority of cases. But poverty has long been recognized as a source of crime.[10]

We also believe that racist attitudes cause racist acts, a belief certainly borne out by the experience of Nazism forty years ago in Germany. Similarly, pornography changes the way a man values a woman; and the way he values a woman affects the way he treats her.

Thus the flow of causality is not that pornography *causes* anti-social or criminal conduct. Rather it is that pornography causes deviant *attitudes* which in turn cause or predispose to anti-social or criminal conduct. In other words, crimes happen more frequently because pornography predisposes criminals to tolerate and even enjoy such anti-social conduct.

How does pornography do this? For one thing, it is enjoyable for the viewer. It is hard for the pornophile to believe—or to care—that what is enjoyable for one person can actually *hurt* another. Thus a record jacket showing a bruised and bleeding still-beautiful woman, tied hand and foot, will have her saying, "I'm black and blue from the Rolling Stones—and I love it." A salacious cartoon will depict a little girl leaving the apartment of a leering sixty-year-old man, with the caption, "And they call *that* child abuse!" In other words, it's *fun*.

Pornography also predisposes to anti-social conduct because, unlike the behavior which it motivates, the depiction does not have unwanted physical consequences in the viewer. Simply to look at pornography, whatever its psychological and moral harm, will not transmit syphilis, gonorrhea, herpes, or AIDS, even though real sex will often incur these consequences. In the make-believe world of autoerotic sex, there is only pleasure, never pain. You always get what you want, and you never get what you do not want. There is always fulfillment, never punishment. For example, in *Super Vixens,* a segment of which was described in the prior chapter, the angry knife-murderer of the oversexed voluptuous shrew hacks her to death and burns her house down, but is never arrested. The "actress" herself returns, unscathed, to portray another sexy villainess untroubled by her unrepentant promiscuity. When he acts out his fantasy, there are no consequences to deter him.

The Corruption of Behavior

If "no girl was ever corrupted by a book," then no girl—or man—was ever ennobled by a book. If what we read and see cannot harm us, no matter how depraved or debased it might be, then what we read cannot improve or uplift us either. If the way books depict women and women's roles did not matter, there would be no point in the current feminist campaign to revise textbook treatment of women.[11] If books did not matter, the rulers of the Soviet Union would not mind if Bibles are shipped in for people to read. If books did not influence people's thoughts, and through those thoughts their attitudes, then Hitler wasted his time writing *Mein Kampf.* As Chief Justice Burger stated correctly:

If we accept the unprovable assumption that a complete education required certain books and the well nigh universal belief that good books, plays and art lift the spirit, improve the mind, enrich the human personality and develop character, can we then say that a state legislature may not act on the corollary assumption that commerce in obscene books, or public exhibitions focused on obscene conduct, have a tendency to exert a corrupting and debasing impact leading to antisocial behavior? [The sum of experience] affords an ample basis for legislatures to conclude that a sensitive, key relationship of human existence, central to family life, community welfare, and the development of human personality, can be debased and distorted by crass commercial exploitation of sex.[12]

Books as such are less the problem these days than magazine photos, action films, video cassettes, and live actions. But these influence attitudes and behavior, just as books do. The widespread public concern about the deleterious effect of television violence on the children's imaginations illustrates the common sense intuition that what we see affects what we do. Indeed, often we act out what we have already seen and approved.

It is instructive to watch the conduct of older teenage boys leaving a theater after viewing a movie glorifying high-speed driving, careening curves, and near-miss turns: the parking lot and sidestreets thunder with gunned motors and shriek with peeled tires. With a gusto born of adulation for the stuntman hero, some will imitate his escapades. Far from their minds is any thought that high speed is dangerous or that the skilled movie driver practices those stunts in slow motion and that those explosive crashes are simulated. High speed is fun to watch and fun to do. It is easy to make the transition from imagination to behavior.

A minority of these viewers will act out the stunt man's driving. Lack of opportunity for some, lack of desire in others, ingrained caution in many, and concern about the radar cop's whereabouts in most will lead most young men to drive reasonably. Yet some will not. And the carefree and careless attitudes they imbibed in the theater may have other consequences. It is only common sense to think that absorption in such visual images, where the civil law and the moral law are violated with impunity, where the violator is depicted favorably, where his violations are shown as pleasurable to him and to the audience—that such imaginative involvement will heighten the spectator's inclination to try it.

So it is with pornography. As Charles Keating and the other dissenters to the Pornography Commission Report showed, and as the testimony of vice squad detectives confirms, in many cases pornography radically changes the attitudes of its devotees. It creates a lawless disrespect for the objects of one's predatory pursuit of pleasure, almost always women and children. It teaches him to treat them in a way spiritually scarcely different from the way a cannibal treats his human captive. It intensifies destructive fantasies and simultaneously breaks down inhibitions against carrying them out. The result often is anti-social behavior. And ''anti-social'' is a bloodless euphemism for what usually happens in sex crimes: we mean child molestation, sexual assault, rape, even murder.

With millions of men stimulating themselves with such fantasies, thousands of men who otherwise would have been more restrained will commit such crimes.

FOUR

Pornography and Crime

ORGANIZED CRIME CREAMS OFF immense profits from pornography. It uses millions of dollars in profits from magazines, movies, and other pornographic "entertainment" to finance narcotics deals and prostitution. Our society will not make much progress in the war against drug abuse, prostitution, and racketeering until we destroy the privileged financial sanctuary that is the pornography money machine.

Michael Stachell, a reporter, stated what is common knowledge in law enforcement circles:

> The porn industry is infested by organized crime, particularly in wholesaling and distribution. Two of the five top leaders, (Mickey) Zaffarano and (Debe) De Bernardo, have been described in federal and state organized crime reports as members of La Cosa Nostra, and mobsters are known to reap vast profits from involvement in the industry or from extortion, pirating films, skimming cash, and payoff agreements under which independent porn merchants pay financial tribute to operate in certain areas.[1]

It is not surprising that the Mafia finds pornography attractive: it makes big money while expending little effort, and it can manipulate a shadow-world clientele of producers, procurers, and purchasers with consciences usually far weaker than their lust for money. The porn merchants will pay it as part of the cost of doing business. Further, there is a natural affinity among the Mafia's products and services. Narcotics pushers, prostitutes, porn producers, and "actresses" all profit from the vice of weak humans willing to break the law to grab some instant pleasure. Indeed, the pay for acting out a hard-core sex scene in a movie frequently is free drugs. And once a young girl becomes a "pony" in a porn producer's "stable," it is a natural—and often coerced—step into prostitution. This is a hard world for all the participants, save perhaps the top people, and many of the participants pay a high price for their moral vagrancy. One newspaper article, entitled "Porn a Risky Business," opened with these two paragraphs suggesting what life is like for porn merchants:

> Murders. Fires. Ties to organized crime. Threatening phone calls. Misrepresentations.
> It has spelled a look-over-your shoulder caution, a frightening concern that has left a group of Kansas Citians tangled in a knot of worries. These are the people involved in a gamut of trades ranging from massage parlors, escort services and pornography to a specialty house offering torture for hire.[2]

With such a high incidence of crime spawned by pornography, the FBI had to do something. A few years ago it set up a complicated infiltration scam by which two undercover agents posed as distributors of videotape pornography. The agents travelled the country getting to know the top producers. The *New York Times,* quoting an FBI source, reported on what they found:

> Every major producer and distributor in the country is in this indictment. We could have indicted 500 people, but we didn't want numbers, we wanted the top people. . . .

The agents. . .attended meetings of top pornographic industry leaders, who convened every six months or so to discuss new products, changes in obscenity laws and other subjects. . . . These meetings resembled small conventions and were held in New Orleans, Las Vegas, Colorado Springs, and Seattle, among other places. . . .

Those from New York indicted were Robert DiBernardo. . .Theodore Rothstein. . .Louis Peraino and Joseph Peraino. . .and Michael Zaffarano. . .

The Peraino Brothers have connections to the Joseph Columbo crime family and provided initial financing for the movie "Deep Throat". . .said a Federal agent. He added that Mr. Zaffarano was once a bodyguard for Joseph C. Bonanno, Sr., and owned adult theaters in New York, Boston, San Francisco and Washington, D.C., and that Mr. DiBernardo. . .was associated with the Scimone crime family in New Jersey.

Among those indicted in other cities were Rubin Sturmin, 54, of Cleveland, who reportedly controls about 300 adult book stores in major cities of the East and Midwest: Harry V. Mohney, 37, of Durland, Michigan, reputedly a major importer of European pornography and the third-largest producer and distributor of pornographic movies, according to law-enforcement officials; and Anthony Arnone, 40, of Plantation, Florida, who once owned 13 adult theaters in south Florida and worked with the Peraino Brothers to gain control of the distribution of the movie "Deep Throat."[3]

The FBI investigation emerged after the evidence of organized crime involvement in pornography had become overwhelming. The Task Force on Organized Crime of the National Advisory Committee on Criminal Justice Standards and Goals had issued an alarming report on the subject in 1976—*five years before* the FBI had amassed enough evidence to bring indictments. The following are some quotes from a summary of the report:

In the Northeast, the report said, "organized crime income. . .is presently invested in a variety of businesses, including. . .massage parlors. . .and pornographic bookstores" and "pornography. . .is showing astronomical distribution profits."

In the Southeast, the report found, "underworld organizations used all variety of business firms," including "massage parlors as fronts for prostitution; and theaters, bookstores, and film companies as fronts for pornography." Tactics used in this area include "arson—particularly in connection with pornography operations," the report said. "Prostitution is frequently linked to drug use and pornography" the report said. "The youthful performers in pornographic films are often paid in drugs for their services, then drawn into prostitution. Books, movies, and peep machines are the most common pornography enterprises; peep machines are the most lucrative. There are signs that organized crime figures from the Northeast and West are involved in pornography in this region, and that it is an extremely profitable and expansive operation.[4]

The report goes on to state that Organized Crime's links to the pornography industry go back to the early 1950s but that massive involvement did not develop until the late 1960s, partly because of legal confusions spawned by court decisions and partly because of the Syndicate's late discovery, in 1978, that the peep shows in Times Square were vastly profitable.

Subjected to typical strong-arm tactics, the owners soon had to give organized crime 50 percent of their profits. From there, it was but a short step to insisting that all outlets use projection machines supplied by organized crime. By 1969, The Colombo family had obtained about 60 percent control of the porno movies in New York.

Organized crime is believed to be in all aspects of the

pornography industry: literature and films of all types (i.e., hard core, soft core, art 16mm, magazines and books), sexual devices, ''service'' establishments (including live sex shows), production, wholesaling and retailing, and distribution.[5]

In an effort to uncover the amount of unreported taxable income the pornography industry produces, New York State authorities undertook a comprehensive investigation in 1970 and followed up every lead or tip indicating racketeering in sex-oriented materials. They checked out the typical ''adult'' book stores, reviewed operating expenses including leases and salaries, magazines, photos, novelties, peep shows, hard core pornography, the live show, and the ''adult'' movie theater. The Commission found the industry made extraordinary profits:

Photos. A section in most book stores was reserved for the sale of what are known as photo sets. These photos typically are packed in cellophane with one photograph visible. Recently these photographs have changed from black and white to color. The earlier photo sets were arranged in a series so as to give the appearance [of]. . .a female undressing. However, they have progressed far beyond this. They currently depict various acts of sexual activity. The kind depicted depends on the purchaser's inclination. These pictures portray either heterosexual, homosexual, or some other activity catered to by that particular store. The profit potential from these photo sets is enormous. These pictures are sold for what the individual clerk feels the traffic will bear, usually in the neighborhood of $8.00 a set, purchased by the bookstore from a distributor for substantially less than 25 cents.[6]

Under the section of ''Hard-core pornography'', the Commission reported:

A reel of color film, commonly called a "stag movie," can be purchased by the store owner for from $2.50 to $3 and can be sold by him for as high as $40. Pornographic playing cards with each individual card depicting a different sexual activity can be produced for about 27 cents a pack. Typically, these packs are sold for $7 to $7.50 each. Photo sets, costing pennies, in black and white, sell for about $6 to $8 in color, for from $1.50 to $2 per photograph. There are usually from 6 to 8 photographs in such a set. The price of magazines varied, depending on whether they were in color or in black and white, from a low of $5 to a high of $12. Most of these items do not have any fixed price but are sold for as much as the clerk feels the traffic will bear. . .[7]

With profit margins as high as 3200 percent, no wonder porn merchants and their customers cast to the winds any sense of frugality or cost-consciousness. As consumer-protection crusaders would say, these are "obscene profits." Nor is it photos alone that generate this kind of money. "Club Orgy," which specialized in live or simulated sex performances also generated unconscionable profits:

This "Club" consisted of a combination sex bookstore—peep show—live show—figure modeling studio. . . . The Club's principal feature was a live show which was staged in a converted loft which seated approximately 150 persons. Featuring simulated sexual intercourse, shows ran from 11 o'clock in the morning to the early hours of the following morning. Admission was obtained by a "membership" payment of $6. The "member" was entitled to remain as long as he wished on the particular day that he had purchased a membership. On leaving, the patron was allowed, free, to select a "nudie-girlie" magazine with a marked price of $3. Actually, these magazines were returns and remains of previous issues, and worth no more than 35 cents apiece.

Up to the time of the Commission's public hearing, at least 2100 arrests charging public lewdness had been made at this premise. However, the Club was able to continue to operate in spite of this concerted police activity because the profit was so great.[8]

The evidence is overwhelming: organized crime is pervasively involved with pornography. It skims off enormous profits to enrich itself, enforce its lawless codes, and procure more performers. It uses this wealth to produce more pornography, in turn generating more wealth, in a truly "vicious" circle. The porn profits pay for other vices as well, chiefly narcotics and prostitution. And it is likely that pornography provides the funds for bribery and other crimes involving public officials. Pornography is for the mob what oil is for OPEC.

Having demonstrated this connection, one would hope the conclusion would be equally obvious: the need for vigorous law enforcement—strong laws, aggressive prosecutors, tough judges—against the pornography racketeers. Unfortunately, some have reached just the opposite conclusion: that the solution to the link between pornography and crime is to "decriminalize" pornography. Civil libertarians on both the left and right would repeal the laws, call off the prosecutors, weaken or remove tough judges from the field.[9]

Of their many fallacious arguments, only one deserves any notice at this point: it is said that pornography attracts the Mafia *because it is illegal.* They argue that if pornography were free and open and available to everybody without a "crime tariff" on what is seen as merely "traffic in a line of commerce," prices would go down and crimes would be reduced in numbers because the suppliers would be driven out of business.[10] Professor Herbert Packer argues:

It is very simply that the conduct in question, whatever else it may be and however heinous we may think it is, is traffic in a line of commerce.

Commerce involves transactions between willing

> buyers and willing sellers, each of whom gets what he
> wants from the deal. By making [this] con-
> duct. . .criminal, what we are in effect doing is limiting
> the supply of the commodity in question by increasing
> the risk to the seller, thereby driving up the price of what
> he sells.[10]

Packer postulates that pornography is a commodity subject to "inelasticity of demand." That is, it is something people want so badly that they don't think much about the price: "something like salt, or medicine, or narcotics."[11] Since the demand for things like narcotics, gambling, abortions, and pornography is inelastic, Packer concludes, all the laws do is create a monopoly for those bold enough to risk the sanctions and thus make huge profits. He thinks that repeal of the laws against narcotics will have beneficial effects: "With the disappearance of controls the price of narcotics would plummet, and the financial ruin of the present illegal suppliers would quickly follow."[12] The same theory would apply to the laws against pornography.

I believe these assertions are outlandish. To liken demand for narcotics to demand for salt or medicine is absurd. The defects in this analogy are obvious. Moreover, to suggest that the demand for narcotics or pornography is "inelastic" denies history and human experience. The demand for these two vices a generation ago was virtually nonexistent compared to the present. Surely the laws, by Packer's own analysis, limit the supplier to "those bold enough." This reduces the number of new and amateur suppliers entering the field. With the total number of new or amateur suppliers lower than it otherwise would be, the number of users is proportionately reduced. Thus those at the margin of the market never enter the group of users, simply because they lack access to the "commodity."

The worst feature of Packer's ersatz economic theory is his assumption that the "disappearance of controls" would make the price of narcotics "plummet," thus causing the "financial ruin" of the "present illegal suppliers." Surely serious students of economics know that in many cases, supply creates demand: as prices drop, former nonpurchasers join the ranks of purchasers. The market expands when great wealth is no longer a precondition of entry. This expansion of the market is precisely what happened in the 1950s when costly television sets dropped in price through competition and mass-production, in the 1960s when pocket calculators became popular, and in the 1970s when cheap digital watches went on sale. It stands to reason that when a commodity sells for $100 per unit fewer people will be able to afford it than when it sells for $50, $25, or $10 per unit.

Professor Packer's prescription for health is to spread the disease around more widely! If the price of a hardcore porn film drops from $100 per print to $25 per print, this change will not bring financial ruin to the mob. The racketeers will simply produce four times as many prints and aggressively market them to new audiences that had been previously inaccessible. Millions of children, young adults, middle-aged, and others are now scarcely touched by pornography because they did not run across it in their local school, on television, or in the hotels with in-house video. With "decriminalization," they will surely be exposed to it.

Though refuted on the merits of sound economics alone, the decriminalizers are also refuted by our actual experience. They argue that laws against pornography do no good, but in practice it has been marginally legal for about fifteen years. By that I mean that the Supreme Court and many lower federal courts have concocted such a mishmash of evidential and definitional rules that many prosecutors will not prosecute. Furthermore, many judges impose only slap-on-the-wrist penalties to convicted pornographers. Thus the kingpins of pornography are able to treat occasional law enforcement pressure as a necessary "cost of doing business." As a practical matter, most of them can count on being left alone most of the time. Further more, what is called "soft core" pornography has been decriminalized for quite some time.

So what has been the result of this "legalization" of pornography? The plague has spread, even as prices remain high. The reason of course is that markets have expanded. A new clientele is inducted as young customers grow into the age where porn becomes interesting. At the same time, the perversion of old clientele intensifies as the pornography producers invent new modes of sexual corruption. One can sell customers a limited number of TV sets, pocket calculators, and digital watches. But the appetite for pornography can become insatiable because it corrupts the *spirit* of a person.

Pornography, Crime, and Urban Decay

The spread of pornography goes hand-in-hand with the spread of urban crime and decay. In every major city where "X-rated" films and "adult" book stores proliferate, the environment reflects their presence: it becomes more dirty, more run-down, more dangerous.

In 1977, the Los Angeles City Department of City Planning, along with other city agencies, conducted a comprehensive study to determine whether the concentration of so-called "adult entertainment" establishments has a blighting or degrading effect on neighborhoods. The term "adult entertainment" was construed to include adult book stores, X-rated theatres, adult motels with X-rated entertainment, massage parlors, sexual therapy establishments (other than those operated by licensed psychologists), and nude, topless, or bottomless bars and restaurants. The result was a lengthy report that should interest everyone concerned about the nation's urban environment.[13]

The Los Angeles City Council directed the Planning Department to carry out a "fact-finding process to determine *whether* adult entertainment establishments, where they exist in concentration, cause blight and deterioration."[14] The report noted that where the question has been posed to the public, "there have frequently been anguished retorts to the effect that 'the answer is so obvious it is ridiculous to even ask the question,' and 'what is the City waiting for before it takes action to eliminate these scourges of society?' "

The Los Angeles Study evaluates the two prime methods cities have used to regulate "adult entertainment" businesses by zoning: the concentration or "Combat Zone" approach, used in Boston, and the dispersal approach, initiated in Detroit.

As to the "Combat Zone" the Study states:

> There has been some indication that it has resulted in an increase in crime within the district and that there is an increased vacancy rate in the surrounding office buildings. Due to complaints of serious criminal incidents, law enforcement activities have been increased. . .[15]

The Los Angeles Police Department found a link between clustering of these establishments in Hollywood and an increase in such serious crimes as homicide, rape, aggravated assault, robbery, burglary, larceny, and vehicle theft. Such crimes increased at nearly twice the rate, during the period 1969 through 1975, in the Hollywood "adult entertainment" area than elsewhere in the city.[16] Other offenses, including incidence of fraud, stolen property, narcotics, prostitution, liquor law violation, and gambling increased even more (45.5 percent in Hollywood, only 3.4 percent in the rest of the city). The most instructive statistic, prostitution arrests, showed the contrast vividly:

> Prostitution arrests in Hollywood Area increased at a rate 15 times greater than the city average. While the city showed a 24.5 percent hike, Hollywood bounded to a 372.3 percent increase in prostitution arrests. . . . Similarly, pandering arrests in the Hollywood area increased by 475.0 percent, 3½ times the city increase of 133.3 percent.[16]

The study also demonstrated that businessmen and residents believe that the concentration of "adult entertainment" has an adverse effect on both the quality of life and on business and property values. Among the harmful business effects cited were difficulty in retaining and attracting customers to non-"adult entertainment" businesses, problems recruiting employees, and problems in renting office space and keeping desirable tenants. Among the adverse effects on the quality of life were: increased crime, the impact on children, neighborhood appearance, litter, and graffiti. In a private poll of residents reported as an appendix to the Study citizens described "adult entertainment" establishments as tawdry, tacky, garish, seedy, messy, neglected, untidy, blighted, and unkempt.

At two public meetings conducted by the Planning Commission, and tape-recorded to insure an accurate record, citizens commented adversely on the spread of sex-related "entertainment" in their neighborhoods. The study recounts citizen complaints about physical deterioration, muggings, offensive signs, and fear of walking the streets at night. A frequent comment noted the type of clientele that "adult entertainment" attracted: persons who rarely patronized traditional business establishments in the area to any significant degree and who often, by their looks and their "lifestyle," repelled such traditional clientele. One person posed the question, "why don't we have an 'Environmental Impact Report' for pornographic businesses?"[17]

Reflections on Crime and Urban Decay

The Los Angeles report—and common sense—suggest that urban crime and decay are closely associated with pornography. Yet in fairness one should consider the skeptic's rejoinder. He will argue that urban blight would not be caused by *legal* sexual entertainments. He will assert that by "criminalizing" sexual entertainments, one creates a vacuum to be filled by the profiteers who operate outside the law. He believes that if pornography and other sex-related entertainments were not outlawed, "outlaws" would not run them.

If running a porn outlet were just one more commercial activity like running a hardware store or a "legit theatre," it would no more promote urban decay than do such traditional businesses.

There are several answers to this objection. First, it misses the point. The claim is that *consumers* of pornography, not the suppliers, commit crimes. If some customers of explicit sexual materials go out and commit sexual assaults, "decriminalizing" the materials that stimulated the assaults will not prevent them. In fact, decriminalizing them will only promote assaults by making the material more widely available and by removing the inhibitions that slightly restrain those tempted to indulge themselves.

Second, adult book stores, massage parlors, X-rated movie houses, and the rest are subject to Mafia infiltration and ultimate control even if they are "legal." The mob has on occasion obtained control over legitimate restaurants and legal casinos. Similarly, it will infiltrate a legal pornography business if mobsters see a potentially high mark-up and consequent immense profits. The fact is that criminals trade on human weakness and make their money out of human vice. Vice is vice, whether it is legal or illegal. The difference is that law enforcement will lose whatever leverage it has over criminals if their involvement in vice is made legal. Without the law enforcement deterrent, the potential to "Expand the market" to new customers is virtually unlimited.

Third, much of the crime associated with the sex-entertainment industry has little to do with which group controls the production and distribution of sexual materials. Rather, these crimes are a function of the amorality the materials teach the customers. The street crimes in Los Angeles that are associated with the sex trade result from the basic moral breakdown and lack of civilized inhibitions pornography and other sex-for-entertainment activities promote. The prostitutes may be under Mafia control, but their "johns"—customers— are not. When the consumer of pornography leaves the theater after stripping his inhibitions away by wallowing in X-rated perversions, and starts down the street toward his parked car only to encounter a prostitute, his defenses are down. Morality, his conscience, vows of fidelity to loved ones, or even the fear of venereal disease are all abstractions swept away by the concrete, immediate prospect of doing, himself, for a few minutes what he has just spent a few hours watching others do.

Pornography breeds crime. It creates predatory attitudes, a ruthless spiritual cannibalism, a habitual mindset of domination and aggression among all its devotees. Consumers of pornography learn to entertain themselves by using women and then tossing them aside.

In some cases, pornography acts as a "how-to-do-it" manual for those inclined to act out their fantasies in sex crimes. It provides enormous profits to the mobsters who control its production and largely direct its wholesale distribution. And the immorality of mind and heart and soul among producer and consumer spreads out like a perverse secular sacrament into external manifestations: neighborhoods decay, legitimate businesses are driven out, long-time residents in and near the new pornography neighborhoods move out or at best hang on in fear and dismay at the increase of street crimes and the perverse influences affecting their children.

In light of this ominous record, it is not an exaggeration to say that the promoters of pornography may well do to modern Western civilization what the assaults of the Barbarians did to the ancient Roman Empire. They may ultimately bring the whole thing down.

FIVE

Psychological Health

WHEN A MAN REGULARLY ENTERTAINS himself with pornography, what happens to his mind? What happens to his consciousness—and his subconsciousness? What happens to the way he looks at life and sex? What will be the quality of psychological health of a man who regularly wallows in pornography? We must consider what happens to a person who spends hours on end, devouring each new issue of the magazines, collecting pornographic films, joining "sex clubs" to watch in someone's bedroom in the instructive orgies in the films and videotapes and magazines.

Let us assume that *this man*—whether lacking opportunity or lacking boldness—never actually commits a pornography-related crime that amounts to acting out the sex-violence fantasies depicted in his pornography collection. Would you still feel comfortable with such a man as a next-door neighbor? Would you still be unconcerned if your daughter went out on a "double date" with two such young men? Would you not be concerned if the "entertainment" at a neighborhood party consisted of viewing the videotape collection owned by the local pornophile?

Most people would be very concerned, for they instinctively grasp essential truths of human psychology that the clinicians have begun to prove empirically. Thus the psychiatrist Frederick Wertham has written:

Negative media effects do not generally consist in simple imitation. They are indirect, long-range, and cumulative, violent images are stored in the brain, and if, when, and how they are retrieved depends on many circumstances. It is a question not so much of attitudes, not of specific deeds, but of personality developments.[1]

One wonders about videocassettes showing sadomasochism when he reads this comment later in Wertham's essay:

The saturation of people's minds with brutal and cruel images can have a long-range influence on their emotional life. It is an effect that involves human relations in fantasy and in fact and can become a contributing factor to emotional troubles and adjustment difficulties.

Though Dr. Wertham's focus was on the long-term influence of viewing television and comic book violence, he expressly applied his findings to the allied field of sexual violence:

With regard to sex, the explicit display of sadomasochistic scenes may have lasting effects. They may supply the first suggestions for special forms or reinforce existing tendencies. The whole orientation of young people with regard to the dignity of women is affected. By showing cruelty with erotic overtones, we teach that there can be pleasure in inflicting pain on others.

What is true of violent sex is also true of scenes of other forms of sex acts. As practitioners of hypnosis have demonstrated, the subject, under hypnosis, can even be made to "regress" to infancy. As he travels back mentally through his personal history, he can recall specific scenes and experiences which had long been dormant in his subconscious. Indeed, believing himself reliving those experiences, he feels many of the same emotions as they originally evoked. Thus Wertham notes that negative media effects are long range and cumulative, that images are *stored* in the brain, that patterns of action are prepared by patterns of thought. If behavior patterns can be shaped by ordinary childhood experiences such as the first day of school or losing a toy, how much more impact will scenes of sexual torture or rape have?

On one level, it is quite true that we never fully forget what we have learned. Visual experiences constantly repeated and reinforced penetrate the subconsciousness and become part of the very psychic being of the person. The clinical psychiatrist Dr. Melvin Anchell has written:

> The adverse effects of audiovisual obscenities permitted in today's entertainment media are sexually devastating to children *and adults*. The belief that pornography is unsuitable mental fare for children but harmless for adults is illogical. It is like saying a human being *suddenly becomes immune to poison at age 18.*[2]

Permanent "Adult" Immaturity

By preoccupying its devotees with infantile fantasies and self-gratification without responsibility, pornography creates a perpetually immature mindset. Young men grow older in body but their outlook remains childish. They are unable to integrate their personalities and put sex—an attractive but partial element of human life—in proper perspective and balance. They never achieve mature adjustment. Dr. Anchell writes that such a person "remains stunted in self-love which is satisfied with immature forepleasures":

> Pornography embellishes the physical sex life of free lovers and perverts who find it difficult to fulfill their complete sexual needs. But complete sexuality is more than a physical relationship. To be life-sustaining, human sexuality must encompass the mind as well as the body. The affectionate component is as important as the physical. Without companionship and affection, the sex act alone

produces frustrations that can lead to serious sexual maladjustments. Free lovers and sexual deviants are in a constant stage of conflict with themselves. They project their conflicts onto others with sadistic vengeance.

The famous social psychologist, Dr. Ernest van den Haag, who is in private practice as a psychoanalyst, asks the rhetorical question, wherein is pornography harmful? He answers with a complementary insight:

> The basic aim of pornographic communication is to arouse impersonal lust. . . . The cravings pornography appeals to—the craving for contextless, impersonal, anonymous, totally deindividualized, as it were, abstract sex—are not easy to control and are, therefore, felt as threats by many persons, threats to their own impulse-control and integration.[3]

Van den Haag says society has even stronger grounds for suppressing pornography than the importance of helping its citizens control impulses which threaten their essential psychic integrity:

> Societies survive by feeling of identification and solidarity among their members, which lead them to make sacrifices for one another, to be considerate and to observe rules, even when they individually would gain by not doing so.

This solidarity, he argues, is cultivated by institutions "which help each of us to think of others not merely as means to his own gratification, but as ends in themselves." One of the shared values these institutions cultivate is the linkage of sexual to individual affectional relations—to love and stability:

> Pornography tends to erode these bonds, in fact all bonds. By inviting us to reduce others and ourselves to purely physical beings, by inviting each of us to regard the other

only as a means to physical gratification, with sensations, but without emotions, with contacts but without relations, pornography not only degrades us (and incidentally reduces sex to a valueless mechanical exercise), but also erodes all human solidarity and tends to destroy all affectional bonds. This is a good enough reason to outlaw it.[4]

Many devotees of pornography become addicts. They collect the magazines and spend countless hours poring over depictions of exaggerated scenes of animal gratification achieved through predatory use of another—usually female—human being. The purpose, it hardly needs saying, is neither "scientific inquiry," nor a noble curiosity about "sex education." It is, to put it bluntly, a psychic cannibalism. The porn addict *identifies with* the super-stud protagonist in the photo or film. He vicariously shares the stud's conquests; he imagines himself doing the same; in his mind he acts out his own fantasies and spurs his imagination through grist for new fantasies. He pretends to be the actor: for a few minutes, or hours, he psychologically *becomes* the actor.

Thus the pornophile takes on the actor's mindset, values, desires, self-image, aggressiveness, lusts. The very purpose of immersing himself in pornography is to "step outside himself," as it were, and step into the role of the depicted rapist, sado-masochist, woman-conquering super-stud.

Thus pornography is escapism. Herein lies much of its appeal: like narcotics, pornography provides a combination of a) escape from the real world, b) escape from inhibitions, c) momentary escape from feelings of personal inadequacy, d) considerable (albeit vicarious) pleasure. It does not take a Ph.D. in psychology to perceive the impact such frequent masturbatory escapism can have on the sense of self-identity of the average teenager. The analogy with hard drugs is instructive. The ego, still amorphous, does not come to grips with reality; it does not define itself through the discipline of self-control in the face of adversity; it seeks fulfillment not through healthy interpersonal relations wherein one might forge common bonds of affection, sharing, love, and sacrifice. The ego seeks its fulfillment in something else.

The Dwarf Psyche

The pornography-saturated ego seeks a counterfeit growth through domination of the anonymous other; its entertainment comes through using and abusing strangers. It withdraws from the structures and patterns of public and civilized society, patterns which, at their best, encourage respect for other persons and a modicum of internal self-discipline.

The porn addict drives a wedge between himself and normal society.[5] He finds it difficult if not impossible to enter relationships with others in which taking pleasure for himself is not the prime consideration. Even when not pursuing vicarious pleasure in his photos and films, he carries with him—imprinted in his nervous system, dominating his imagination, absorbing any surplus time and energies, distracting his concentration—the urge, the desire, the lust for *more*. He has surrendered to his appetite for sex. He becomes, it is not an exaggeration to say, little more than an animal perpetually in heat. He stalks the streets looking for sexual outlet.

This accurate analysis hits harder when made concrete. Therefore I will excerpt comments by Dr. Melvin Anchell, the Los Angeles psychiatrist, about one of his cases. Dr. Anchell tried, with limited success, to restore a young man he calls "Marty" to some mental balance, after he had become thoroughly addicted to pornography.

Marty, age 17, came to me for treatment of his recurrent headaches. My experience as a father and a physician practicing psychiatry has given me a certain rapport with teenagers; and it was not long before Marty discussed with me his real problem.

It had begun four years previously when Marty was in junior high. The son of affluent, professional parents, he was not only a bright student but was popular as well. One afternoon another 12-year-old boy invited Marty and a group of school-mates, boys and girls, to come to his home to view a movie which his parents showed at grownup parties. Since every young person's ambition is to prove that he can act like an adult, he had an eager audience while he played host during his parents' absence.

The movie turned out to be hard-core pornography, graphically depicting sexual intercourse along with every type of perversion. After the initial embarrassment, the majority of the children were completely seduced. They attempted to outdo the adults in the movie then and there.

By the time he entered high school, Marty told me, his earlier promiscuity had ceased because he no longer "got a kick out of it." His problem, he said, was that he was impotent. For sexual stimulation, he now needed drugs. At present, he is a school dropout, finding release in drug-induced sexual fantasies.

Is there any hope for Marty to return to a normal life? It is most improbable. You cannot stretch the bones of a dwarf. A dwarf's subnormal size is due to premature closure of the bones in childhood. Marty's impotence was due to his sexual growth having been stunted before mature development occurred in adolescence. . . .

There is no practical way for our society to accept responsibility for tragedies comparable to Marty's which abdication indirectly causes:

Marty's experiences with pornography sated him with sex before the process of idealization was established in his relations with girls. As a result he holds girls in contempt. His unresolved affectionate longings have built up a continuous succession of frustrations. His bitterness and disappointment with carnal sex devoid of spiritualization have created such a reservoir of hate for females that his sadism is almost fiendish. He has gradually reverted to satisfying physical sexual needs entirely through voyeurism and sadism. His greatest delight is in having orgastic responses after beating his female cohorts. Sadistic pleasures have spilled inwardly into himself, and he is gradually destroying his life with drugs.[6]

This is a true story. Marty was a victim of pornography. An unnecessary victim. His case proves that *it does matter how people entertain themselves.*

Marty's story is one that lax laws against pornography will multiply thousands of times around the country. It demonstrates the downhill spiral: the addict constantly seeks new "highs," more bizarre titillation. It also is an ironic and sad story. At a time when the states and federal government are spending more money than ever before to promote "mental health," the Justice Department has been very slow to use the laws now on the books to prosecute the pornographers, whose product preys on the mental health of all our children. Perhaps the government which subsidizes both the growing of tobacco and research on cancer will increase its appropriations for mental health to address the psychological problems of pornography addicts. Regrettably, after-the-fact palliatives will not cure the moral contamination typified by Marty's case and others like it.

Pornography as a Teacher of Aggression

There is a certain type of pornography that promotes especially anti-social behavior. This is what some writers call "aggressive erotica." It blends sexual stimulation with violent depiction in such a way that the pleasure of viewing each reinforces the other.

It is not easy to determine the causal link between viewing sadomasochistic erotica and actual erotic aggression such as rape, sexual assault, sexual torture, and piquerism. As was discovered in some of the Obscenity Commission's empirical studies, obtaining a "control group" and isolating the stimuli under laboratory conditions are difficult. Still, some skilled researchers have undertaken the task with methodological care and they have come up with defensible results.

One such study was reported by Edward Donnerstein in the *Journal of Personality and Social Psychology*.[7] The author, then a visiting professor in the psychology department at the University of Wisconsin, sought to examine the effects of aggressive-erotic stimuli on male aggression toward females. In the experiment, 120 male subjects were angered or treated in a neutral manner by a male or female confederate. The researchers then showed the subjects either a neutral, and erotic, or an aggressive-erotic film and gave them an opportunity to aggress against the male or female by delivering an electric shock. Results indicated that the aggressive-erotic film was effective in increasing aggression overall, and it produced the highest increase of aggression against the female. Even nonangered subjects showed an increase in aggression toward the female after viewing the aggressive-erotic film.

In another clinical setting, researchers Seymour Feshback and Neal Malamuth of UCLA developed comparable evidence. They summarized their experiments and findings in an article in *Psychology Today*.[8]

One of their experiments is summarized thus:

> To determine whether aggression can be bad for sex, we studied reactions to portrayals of one of the most violent sex acts: rape. . . .we compared the reactions of a number of college undergraduates to varied erotic and rape passages we had adapted from books. We found, indeed, that reading about a rape generally inhibited the sexual responses of both men and women. But the responses depended quite a bit on whether the victim was described as being in pain and whether she finally

succumbed to—and enjoyed—the act. From women, high pain cues resulted in low sexual arousal, regardless of whether the victim ultimately gave in. *For men, however, the fantasy of a woman becoming sexually excited as a result of a sexual assault reversed any inhibitions that might have been mobilized by the pain cues and by the coercive nature of the act. This finding is particularly worrisome if, as writers such as Susan Brownmiller have emphasized, the typical rape story in pornographic books and magazines portrays the women as sexually aroused during the act.*

A perennial problem for psychologists has been the difficulty of measuring non-laboratory stimuli. How, for instance, do neighborhood movies affect the viewers' inclination toward violence?

While at the University of Manitoba, Neal Malamuth sent hundreds of students to local movies that portrayed sexual violence as having positive consequences. He sent them to films usually considered *less* shocking than pornography: everyday "sex and violence" of the R-rated variety. The films included *Swept Away* (about a violent male aggressor and a woman who learns to crave sexual sadism, who find love on a deserted island), and *The Getaway* (about a woman who falls in love with the man who raped her in front of her husband, both then taunting the husband till he commits suicide). Dr. Malamuth assigned a second group of students to see two control films, *A Man and a Woman* and *Hooper* (showing tender romance and nonexplicit sex). Within a week he administered an attitude survey to all the students without their knowing the survey had anything to do with the films they had seen. Embedded within the survey were questions about the acceptance of interpersonal violence and about rape myths such as "women enjoy being raped."

The results of the survey indicated that exposure to the films showing violent sexuality significantly increased male subjects' acceptance of interpersonal violence against women.[9]

There is also evidence that exposure to non-aggressive erotic materials "desensitizes" the viewers: that is, the materials become less offensive and objectionable. Drs. Dolf Zillman and Jennings Bryant at Indiana University studied 160 male and female undergraduates who were divided into three groups. The first was exposed to massive amounts of pornography over six weeks; the second to a moderate amount over that time period; and the third to no pornography during the period. They found that those viewing massive amounts were desensitized; they also tended to see rape as a more trivial offense and, even without seeing aggressive pornography, they had an increasing loss of compassion for women as rape victims. In a word: pornography caused callousness among men.[1]

In light of the mounting clinical evidence that pornography distorts male psychology, it is not surprising that even civil libertarians are beginning to think something must be done. Thus A.C.L.U. staff attorney Marjorie Smith quotes with approval a statement by the feminist group, Women Against Violence Against Women (WAVAW), decrying billboards and record album covers glorifying sex-nuanced assaults on women: "We think it's harmful in that it contributes to the overall environment that romanticizes, trivializes, and even encourages violence against women"; and urges the record industry to "demonstrate the same sensitivity to women that it has shown in racist advertising and advertising that glorifies drug usage."[11]

Another feminist, Susan Brownmiller, summed up the case fairly well:

What we object to is the sexual humiliation and degradation of women that is *the essence of pornography*. Pornography's intent is a call of violence against the female body. We object to the presentation of rape, torture, mutilation, and murder for erotic stimulation and pleasure.[12]

Pornography and Hate

In the incisive article which suggested the title of this section, the British literary critic and poet David Holbrook, states that the depersonalization of sex for commercial purposes represents a "militant and malicious assault on human values," which can be likened to "a sexual fascism."[13] He supports such characterization by noting that pornographic images and words create an intense mental concoction of often brutal imagery: they make woman into a commodity-thing. She is humiliated and subjected to contempt as a mere sex object:

> In her image, humanity itself is degraded, by being deprived of value and subjected to hate, as the Jew or Negro is degraded in racist propaganda. . . . Pornography creates a fantasy of aggressive humiliation, and of submission, very much akin to the dynamics of the pogrom. This is why it is fascistic. . . .it combines the urge both to control and exploit others. . . .

Just as someone who hates has nothing in common with the object of his hate, so the protagonist in a pornographic film has nothing in common with the person whose body he uses for momentary erotic pleasure and then discards. Even in "consenting-adult" pornographic displays, the actor and actress (if one may be euphemistic) come together not for each other but for the camera. Their common bond, at best, is money. There is no mutual respect, there is no tender concern; there is only exploitation.

Pornography makes the exploitation of others socially acceptable. It expresses and glamorizes the inability of the pervert to enter into a creative love relationship. It is a form of counterfeit education: it *teaches* us to substitute mere sexuality for meaningful love, to seek fulfillment in the momentary pleasure of controlling the sex-object who is dominated by the passions unleashed by the protagonist, who in turn *represents* the male viewer for whom he is surrogate.

True love seeks the good of the other. It seeks to ennoble him or her, to raise him or her up, to share the other's needs and aspirations by affirming that other as a unique and valuable individual person. Love always seeks to dignify and respect the other. Yet as Joseph Sobran writes:

> As the increasing tendency to feature women and even children in debased and deviant activities suggests, the appetite for pornography is in large part an appetite, and an insatiable one, for human indignity, for the tearing away of protective veils and manners, for the violation of personality.[14]

Pornography reduces the body and person to a mere bearer of sensation. By "leaving nothing to the imagination" it destroys human vision. In the process it undermines empathy and the capacity to care for others as the persons they really are. By its pitiless concentration on self-pleasure, it diminishes mutual self-respect, promotes mental rage, corrupts feelings, and isolates its devotees and victims in the doorless chamber of their own minds.

SIX

Exploitation of Women

PORNOGRAPHY IS A MALE OBSESSION. Until recently, scarcely any women have been writers of pornography. The classic pornographic depiction, which is still the backbone of the genre, depicts sexual activity with the man as the protagonist. Almost all of the audience at pornographic films are men. If women are present, usually it is because men have brought them along—a strange way to entertain a lady, but perhaps reflective of modern confusions about entertainment. Pornographic magazines pander to male readers: the ads are oriented to male tastes; the stories to male interests; the photos of nude females in provocative poses are clearly designed to "turn a man on."[1]

Pornography feeds twisted male fantasies about women. Invariably the pornographic film or photo shows a beautiful woman vulnerable and available to be *used*, roughly, by the male with whom the viewer identifies. The woman often appears to enjoy and even want this treatment. The message is: women are men's playthings, their toys for instant gratification, immediate pleasure—and equally instant disposal.

In more bizarre forms of obscenity, such as piquerism (stabbing, to relieve the sexual urge and cause pleasure), "snuff" films (in which the unsuspecting "actress" is *literally killed* at the height of orgasm), and how-to-do-it scenes of rape, the viewer wallows in primitive destructive emotions: a subhuman mixture of aggression, anger, lust, and domination. The woman is made to appear no more than a function or an organ. The camera's focus and interest is solely genital: it is irrelevant *who* this person is; any woman would do, as long as her physical attributes are exaggerated. She has no value in herself; her only value and purpose is for the male. She is quite simply an object. She is a thing. This is true even if the pornography is not explicitly violent. Pornography that is not overtly violent is still implicitly violent because it objectifies and degrades women.[2]

What is surprising is the readiness, at least until recently, of women as a class to be used for these purposes. There seem to be no limits to the steady stream of nubile maidens who will trade their beauty for money by accepting pay for doing before the camera acts only twenty years ago thought appropriate, if at all, only in the bedroom. Nor, again until recently, did feminists realize the antithesis between their "sexual liberation" goal and the sexual exploitation through pornography consequent upon that "liberation." It may be that avant-garde women believe differences between the sexes are almost entirely due to cultural conditioning, and do not realize that men are made differently, that, in most cases, men will react far more aggressively than women to the cumulative attitudes instilled by pornography.

Fantasy and Reality

In the standard pornographic film, a man aggressively takes a woman. Often she acts helpless, unable to stop him, unable to control her own desires which (the film suggests) overcome her will and work in concert with his advances. In the last few years, violence has become a dominant theme: the man's advances overcome active resistance, he uses whips or chains, he ties down the woman. Sadomasochism combines with sex.

Thousands of young and middle-age men are entertaining themselves with such fantasies. By identifying with the protagonists, they vicariously enact his assault. They enjoy momentary sexual thrills to the degree that their imagination, stimulated by the magazine or movie pictures, can "relive" or "simultaneously-live" what they watch. To understand the educational import of such fantasy, a comparison is apt.

Many airlines educate their pilots, at one stage in their flight training, on a "simulator." This is a complicated device like a "pretend cockpit": a mock-up of the pilot's cabin, complete with controls, sounds, even the pull of gravity (to some degree) and diagonal tilt, combined with films that create the visual impression of typical flight situations, such as landing in a rainstorm. By putting the pilot into the "real" situation with high degree of verisimilitude, the trainer conditions him to respond with appropriate judgment under real-life stress. To "do a dry run" in the imagination enables an actor to "play the role" more completely when he steps into a comparable setting in real life.

Pornography is a comparable trainer. It gives its devotees easy conquest in the imagination, conditioning them to seek easier conquest in reality. However, pornography is even more successful in breaking down the usual barrier between fantasy and reality because of its peculiar attraction. Unlike flight simulation or other pretend games, pornography can use the male's natural propensity toward sex to bridge the gap between image and reality. Males, especially young men, day-dream about sex and often consciously define self-worth in terms of real or imagined sexual prowess. Their unruly chemistry is always ready to erupt at the presence of sexual stimulation. Thus pornographic portrayals affect both the viewer's grasp of reality and the viewer himself. He is changed, temporarily by his momentary arousal as he engages in autoerotic masturbation, more permanently by the cumulative residue of images stored up in his memory and even his subconscious.

The Educational Impact of Pornography

Modern students of the impact on children of watching repeated scenes of violence are amassing evidence that such depictions gradually dull the moral sensibility and have a seriously negative effect. One of the earlier studies was by the psychiatrist Frederic Wertham, who concluded that sadoerotic crime comics have a negative effect on children:

> The most subtle and pervading effect of crime comics on children can be summarized in a single phrase: moral disarmament. I have studied this in children who do not commit overt acts of delinquency, who do not show any of the more conspicuous symptoms of emotional disorder and who may not have difficulty in school. The more subtle this influence is the more detrimental it may be. It has an influence on character, on attitude, on the higher functions of social responsibility, on super-ego formation, and on the intuitive feeling for right and wrong. . .[It] consists chiefly of a blunting of the finer feelings of conscience, of feeling for other people's suffering and of respect for women as women and not merely as sex objects to be bandied around or as luxury prizes to be fought over.[3]

That the images we allow into our minds do substantially influence our overt acts is a well-known fact. Social psychologists have spent considerable efforts studying the influence of violence on television. Their findings are well known: in sum, there is a measurable correlation between children and adolescents' viewing of TV violence and their own real-life aggression and heightened propensity toward violence. In some cases, children actually imitate the acts they see on television. Researchers McLeod, Atkin, and Chaffee concluded, for instance:

> Our research shows that among both boys and girls at two grade levels (junior high and senior high) the more the child watches violent television fare, the more aggressive he is likely to be. . .Adolescents viewing high levels

of violent content on television tend to have high levels of aggressive behavior, regardless of television viewing time, socio-economic status, or school performance.[4]

It goes without saying that children, even senior high school students, are not adults; and violence is not sexual activity. But when one considers the psychological mechanisms at work in both types of depiction and for both types of person, young and not-so-young, he must wonder whether these differences really matter. In both cases exciting action is shown. In both cases the viewer tends to identify with the actor. In both cases the harmful consequences of the acts (injury, venereal disease) are not given. In both cases the moral dimension of the human interaction is neglected. Both cases provide "escape." There is pleasure, vicarious to be sure, in both types of viewing. The temptation to imitate is present in both: if watching is fun, doing is even more fun.

So too with the similarities between the two groups: age eighteen is no magic watershed, before which one is "immature," after which he is "mature." Many if not most rapes and sexual assaults are committed by men over eighteen; and every person, no matter his age, can have his attitudes modified if he immerses himself in prolonged watching of violence or raw sex. A man's attitudes about women become coarse and debased if he fills his daydreams with coarse and debased fantasies showing the pleasure in mistreating them. A man who entertains himself with images of sexual violence against women attends a "school" different from civilizing experiences that build normal character.

In this connection, the American Civil Liberties Union magazine, *The Civil Liberties Review*, contained the highly pertinent article, " 'Violent Pornography' and the Women's Movement."[5] The essay summarizes the founding and work of a feminist group called Women Against Violence Against Women (WAVAW) which grew out of organized opposition to the showing in Los Angeles. . .of "snuff"—a film that depicted as entertaining the murder and mutilation of a woman. The article describes WAVAW as

'an activist organization working to stop the gratuitous use of images of physical and sexual violence against women in mass media—and *the real world violence against women it promotes. . .'*

and quotes a member:

We think it's harmful in that it contributes to the overall environment that romanticizes, trivializes, and even encourages violence against women.

The author, an ACLU staff attorney, observes:

WAVAW probably cannot demonstrate that particular media portrayals are directly responsible for antisocial conduct, although *it is not irrational to believe that the offending material may well have harmful effects.* As WAVAW claims: 'When millions of people see women portrayed as victims day in and day out, an impression is created that women *are* victims, that it's safe, OK and in fact normal to pick on women. . .Furthermore, a lot of record advertising uses images of violence to women in a joking. . .manner—which. . .trivializes and demeans the very real pain that raped and battered women suffer. . .' (Emphasis added)

It is encouraging to see a serious libertarian journal publishing an article which acknowledges that still photos, even, on mere billboards and record-album covers, can promote actual violence in "the real world" and that it is socially important to worry about the "overall environment."

Feminist writers have begun to discern the educational dimension of pornography and the vicious way it promotes hostility against women. Andrea Dworkin, author of a book titled *Women-Hating,* has called the explosion of pornography "the new terrorism."[6] Leah Fritz, a feminist author who once worked for *Screw* magazine, said that she now is convinced the "pornography is nothing less then gynocidal propaganda."[7] Another feminist speaking at a symposium stated:

Violent porn. . .portrays women as victims and depicts violence against women as permissible or entertaining. . .As the surrounding environment becomes inundated with violent porn, our society comes to accept the view that women are objects to be brutalized. . .The most disturbing aspect of violent pornography is that it serves to reinforce and mold adult behavior. Men come to feel that it is perfectly acceptable to victimize or brutalize women. It is dangerous for men to have the dehumanized view of sex which results from viewing pornography. It distorts their image of women and debases them as well.[8]

In an essay titled *Pornography's Part in Sexual Violence,* Andrea Dworkin impassionately wrote:

. . .pornography *is* violence against women: the women used in pornography. Not only is there a precise symmetry of values and behaviors in pornography and in acts of forced sex and battery, but in a sex-polarized society men also learn about women and sex from pornography. The message is conveyed to men that women enjoy being abused. Increasingly, research is providing that sex and violence—and the perception that females take pleasure in being abused, which is the heart of pornography— teach men both ambition and strategy.

In addition to common sense conclusions and empirical research, there is the evidence of testimony: women coming forth to testify to the role that pornography played in their own experiences of sexual abuse. One 19-year-old woman testified at a Hartford trial [at which Ms. Dworkin was an expert witness] that her father consistently used pornographic material as he raped and tortured her over a period of years. She also told of a network of her father's friends, including doctors and lawyers, who abused her and other children. One of these doctors treated the children to avoid being exposed.[9]

One sign of women's growing concern about pornography was the fact that the editors of *Family Circle* magazine, which rarely deals with social policy issues, published an article on the subject in February 1981.[10] After endorsing a description of pornography as "images and writing that objectifies and degrades its subject for the purpose of sexual stimulation or entertainment," the authors declare bluntly that pornography does have harmful educational influence:

Pornography hurts all women by portraying them only as sexual objects. And it hurts men and boys as well, especially those who are exposed to pornography at an early age, by giving them a limited, leering view of women. In sum, pornography damages everyone in our society.

The authors then discuss the "catharsis theory" of pornography, which holds that pornography prevents sex crimes because it gives the pornophile a "release" for his pent-up rage against women. They reject this theory because it implies that men have naturally sick views of women. It also carries implicit "sexual blackmail," that is, the catharsis notion it seems to be saying to women: "Allow us to picture a *few* of you being degraded and violated in fantasy so that *most* of you will be spared the same fate in reality."

The *Family Circle* authors think the opposite of the catharsis theory is true, namely, that a man is more likely to commit a sex crime if he is immersed in pornography. As we have seen, research shows that males become more aggressive and prone to sexual violence after exposure to violent pornography.[11] The authors conclude with a summary of what pornography teaches men:

> Looking at today's pornography, it is clear that it communicates a number of distorted lessons which color basic attitudes about women and sex. Of these lessons one of the most obvious and harmful is that there's nothing out of the ordinary about brutalizing women and children. Pornography's overwhelming message is always that the victim isn't really a person but simply an object to be used.
>
> Another implicit and dangerous lesson is that women *love* to be raped, beaten and degraded. In a study of pornographic novels, sociologist Don Smith found that the stories depicting rape initally focused on the victim's pain and terror, but her pain and terror were nearly always transformed into unleashed sexual passion.
>
> Photographs and films also communicate the idea that forced sex is always eventually fun for the victim . . . . Perhaps most frightening, pornography teaches that whether or not girls and women desire and delight in rape and battery, they *deserve* such treatment. Richard Snowden. . .has found that it frequently depicts women as inherently evil creatures that need to dominate and do harm to men.

The message seems to be getting through to the Women's Movement: pornography radically debases women. Consider these images from slides shown at a symposium at New York University Law School:

> . . .cover of a record album, *Wild Angel:* a woman with her head thrown back, throat exposed, chain through her mouth, like the bit used to break horses. . .

. . .from the magazine *Roped and Raped:* woman nude, bound and gagged. . .

. . .album called *Pleasure* by the Ohio Players: a black female model. . .wrists chained together and suspended above her head. The woman looks dehumanized; her head is shaved.[12]

Such images bring home the fundamental fact about pornography: it teaches that there is enjoyment in exploiting and dehumanizing women. It caters to an imagination that is or will soon become misogynist; it destroys respect, affection, warmth, caring, and love. It depicts women treated as animals. Indeed, it is illegal to treat dogs and cats in the way women are treated in pornography. As Ernest van den Haag notes:

By inviting us [men] to reduce others [women] and ourselves to purely physical beings, by inviting each of us to regard the other only as a means to physical gratification, with sensation but without emotions, with contacts but without relations, pornography not only degrades us but also erodes all human solidarity and tends to destroy all affectional bonds. This is a good enough reason to outlaw it.[13]

Women's Bondage and Women's Liberation

Feminists are objecting to pornography, but their understanding of the problem is still incomplete. At the NYU Colloquium, Susan Brownmiller, the feminist author, summed up the feminist case this way:

What we object to is the *sexual humiliation and degradation of women* that *is the essence of pornography*. Pornography's intent is call of violence against the female body. We object to the presentation of rape, torture, mutilation, and murder for erotic stimulation and pleasure.

This is not exactly the point. Indeed, Ms. Brownmiller and the other feminists seem torn between their rightful concern about the anti-female essence of pornography and their "libertarian" inclination to absolutize the First Amendment. Further, their focus on the degradation of women seems to overlook the fact that pornography also degrades children of both sexes and degrades young men as well (homosexual pornography). One suspects that some feminists at least would tolerate other forms of pornography if only *women* could be factored out of pornographic pictures and films. To put it another way, their concern is *specific* and not *generic*. Feminists do not fully discern the common thread that connects all forms of pornography.

This common thread is predatory hedonism. At root, pornography is the glorification of what one might call "psychological cannibalism"—the use of women, children, and boys for all the pleasure they can disgorge in a passing encounter. Though violent pornography against women deserves women's concern, the issue is deeper: pornography of *any* kind deserves *every* civilized citizen's concern. For all pornography does the same thing: it tells the viewer to take pleasure for its own sake, to cast off all moral and cultural restraints, to treat another human as a thing, not a person. As such, it is a threat not only to women in our civilization; it is a threat to our civilization itself.

Feminists should also reflect on the implications of the sexual "liberation" that seems to be part of their program. Few can argue with the principle, "Equal pay for equal work." Yet a by-product of feminism is the notion that women should have the same opportunity as men to be sexually promiscuous. Women as a group see themselves as less valuable than they once did, as less worthy of the strict codes of chaste courtship that most of their mothers and probably all of their grandmothers preferred. Many young women are willing to embrace a barracks-room attitude toward sex. "My place or yours?" is the usual conclusion to a flirtatious singles bar encounter.

The sexually liberated lifestyle may be more the fantasy of Hollywood television writers than the usual practice of women.

Yet is there not a connection between the sexual "liberation" of women and the current explosion of pornography and exploitative sexual activity?

There surely is such a connection and, towards the end of the 1970s, many feminists began to see it. They did not like where they were heading. In freeing women from sexual restraints they had reinforced the male pressures for erotic "freedom" as well. And men were not being gentlemen about it. The billboards and record jackets started appearing, showing half-dressed women tied and beaten, bruised, sometimes bloody, yet smiling through it all. Women reported that men were acting out the sadistic fantasies their pornography lessons taught them. Though many feminists did not like to admit it, they had started to do what the two doctors in Dr. Frankenstein's laboratory had done: create a monster.

Feminists who campaign against pornography have not yet embraced a traditional view of public morality and public decency. They should. They should also develop a more comprehensive understanding of the nature of pornography. Pornography exploits women whether the depicitions are violent or voluntary, for it makes women no more than a foil, an organ, a function, with nothing personal or unique or lasting in the encounter. The pornographer portrays sex too closely to make it an art and he removes its sacred and personal character. Even non-violent pornography with women depicted exploits women. It should be obvious, especially to feminists who see the point elsewhere, that when you are exploited you are not "liberated."

SEVEN

Exploitation of Children

LEO IS A SUCCESSFUL SALESMAN. This is how he relaxes when he gets to a new city:

When I arrive at a city on my itinerary, the first thing I do is check into my hotel, have a leisurely lunch or dinner, and then if I know any one in town, decide whether I want to make a few calls to boys I'm already friendly with or make some new friends. Usually I'll decide to get in the car and go cruising. Just about every sizable American city has cruising areas, and I know all the ones in my territory, which pretty much covers the eastern seaboard. I'll cruise the local bus stop first, then head for the penny arcade or the bowling alley—wherever they hang out. Inevitably I'll find a boy. When I look over the pickings, I go for the aesthetic type. I prefer them clean-cut, about thirteen or fourteen, just starting their growth spurt, sincere and bookish.

If we pretend I'm just giving him a lift, there's a good deal of nonverbal communication from the moment he gets in—things like how far away from me he sits, how he looks at me, whether our hands touch. Then we negotiate the price. Usually the kid comes out with something he needs, like a new tire for his bike—that's ten dollars—or a new shirt or a pair of pants for twenty dollars or so. After that things move pretty quickly. I'm not interested in prolonging it—as soon as I've got my money's worth I say good night. Sometimes, if I'm interested in seeing the boy again, I'll take his number before I drop him off just in case I hit a dry spell the next time I'm in town, although that hasn't happened yet. But most of the boys I deal with aren't really very much interested beyond the evening any more than I am.

If I'm satisfied, I then drive back to my hotel, have a few drinks, and call it a night. Or sometimes if the evening is still young and the kid wasn't enough for me, I'll go out and find another.[1]

The prostitution/pornography industry has swallowed up hundreds of thousands of little children in the last decade. Many are lured in when barely beyond kindergarten, at ages five to eight. Most are burned out well before they are eighteen. If their bodies survive countless sexual encounters, their souls do not. As one writer said, "It is the most inhuman of crimes. For pleasure and profit, pornographers have murdered the childhood of a million girls and boys, victims who must live with the dreadful memories of their experience."[2]

Consider these actual cases; the children involved are—or were—real children. They started life with the same innocence and promise as your children. Indeed, unless society demands tough law enforcement, they may well be your children in a few years.

Case: The 17-year-old boy is in bad shape. He has syphilis, ulcers, intestinal parasites, lice. He is alcoholic. He tells the priest that he has been a male prostitute for three years, that he has survived by hustling on the streets of New York City. He has sold himself in perhaps a thousand beds and a thousand cars. He does not like what he knows of life, and he challenges the priest to tell him why he should not jump off a bridge.[3]

Case: Veronica, an eleven-year old girl, was arrested for prostitution eight times, yet the authorities never bothered to determine her age. Each time her pimp paid her $100 fine and put her back on the street. Veronica was thrown out of a tenth-story window and killed, by either her pimp or a customer shortly after her twelfth birthday.[4]

Case: With the bait of child stardom in a movie to be called "Susan's Magic Carpet," a weekly $1,800 salary, and a round-the-world trip, seven sets of well-meaning and ambitious parents permit their grammar-school-age girls to do "brief nude scenes" on camera at the home of a "producer," who collects and sells thousands of "Kiddie porn" photographs.[5]

Case: A twenty-two-year-old man is convicted of kidnapping and murdering an eight-year-old child and of kidnapping and raping a ten-year-old child; at trial he testifies that one of the girls "reminded me of a girl in a pornographic book."[6]

Child Pornography

Child pornography first began to appear at adult bookstores in the late 1960s. Its purveyors started their guerrilla attack on the dominant "straight" culture's values with cautious sorties. Much of the early child porn was fake, with young women dressed like children, posing suggestively among toys or playgrounds. Or the pedophiles—and those who would profit from incipient pedophilia—would use younger teenage girls whose exact age was hard to tell but whose sexual vulnerability was hard to miss.

We have done virtually nothing to stamp out this pandering to a type of lust which, until the last twenty years, every society had deemed beneath contempt. By the latter half of the 1970s, more than 260 different magazines featured children engaged in sexual acts or otherwise posing lasciviously. Among the better known were *Moppets*, filled with photos of wide-eyed little girls from three to eight years old; *Lollitots*, with child models from eleven to fourteen; and *Chicken Brats*, with young boys, appealing to homosexuals. Others included *Perverse Kinder. . .Children Love. . .*and *Fetish Times*.

By 1976, obscenity dealers carried immense quantities of photos and films of children aged three to sixteen in every conceivable sexual pose and act. There are "underground newspapers" which typically print more than thirty ads for sexual materials on a single page, more than half of which are for child pornography.[7]

Adult bookstores began to show "loops" of child pornography. These are short two-minute film segments that can be viewed for about a quarter. One of the most popular loops ever shown was called *First Communion*. This is a description by Clifford L. Linedecker in his definitive study of the child pornography industry, *Children In Chains*:

> One of the most popular loops ever shown was *First Communion*. The film opens with several little girls in crisp white dresses receiving their First Communion. The ceremony is barely underway when a motorcycle gang barges into the church. Gang members beat the priest, chain him, and crucify him on the cross above the altar. Then they turn on the terrified children, rip off their clothes, and rape them. The film is silent, and the screams of the girls can't be heard, but their terror appears real. And their blood appears real.[8]

There are people in the United States who film such horrors—and many others who entertain themselves by watching them. This one film alone seared the imaginations of thousands of young and middle aged men with emotional pleasure associated with raping little girls. Its teaching was clear: it is *fun* to rape seven-year-old virgins.

Some months after reading about *First Communion* I debated Larry Flynt on television and learned that his magazine carried a regular cartoon feature, "Chester the Molester," which glorified child molesting. I found out that *Hustler* magazine also featured advertisements for vinyl/rubber life-like child size boy and girl dolls, complete with sexual parts, and capable of copulating mechanically.

A scholarly expert in child pornography, Dr. Ann W. Burgess of Boston University School of Nursing, estimates that "There are nearly 280 magazines on the market dealing with child pornography, and of these, 275 are published monthly. In each of these editions there are estimated to be 800 to 1000 additional suppliers of child pornography for sale to the subscriber." Burgess and her co-authors have described the devious lengths "private syndicates" (sex clubs) go in their effort to circulate pictures of youngsters, preparatory to arranging to procure the child in person:

> The use of the mail system enables syndicate members to send photos and films of children all over the country, as well as to foreign countries. Many child pornographic operations use post office boxes and fictitious names. For example, if the main operation was based in Chicago, the buyer of now illegal and hard-to-obtain commercially published child pornography would send his response to Sweden or Germany. The mail received by a forwarding agent overseas is opened, cash or checks placed in a Swiss bank account, and the order remailed under a different cover back to the United States. Two reasons for this procedure: 1) the subscriber does not know where the operation originates, and 2) local law enforcement will have a difficult time tracing the operation.[9]

Reliable estimates suggest that more than 500,000 children are involved nationally, at any one time, in various forms of prostitution and pornography. Counting those no longer directly involved because they are burned out or have graduated to other forms of crime such as drug dealing, and those marginally implicated but leaving no identifiable trail, it is accurate to conclude that this subculture of vice touches more than one million minors. Father Ritter's Covenant House accepts 20,000 children per year alone, but this figure does not reveal how many more children are out there on the streets unaware of this single shelter, or those unwilling or unable to run the risk of reprisal if they seek help in the "straight" world. Ruthless pornographers employ trickery, manipulation, and sheer coercion to recruit and keep young people.[10]

The Damage to Children

A psychiatrist with a lifetime of clinical experience treating sexually maladjusted children and adults sums up the impact of child promiscuity this way:

A child crawls before he walks. He does not naturally or normally try to walk, or even stand erect, until his bones and muscles are sufficiently developed to carry his weight in the upright position. If his parents force him to walk before he is naturally prepared to do so, the child's legs will become permanently bowed. The effect of "forced" or premature experiences in a child's sexual development is even more damaging. The child naturally progresses through various stages of sensual awareness from infancy to adulthood. If he is introduced to mature sexual experiences before his mental apparatus is ready to cope with them, he may—like the child who learns to walk prematurely—develop a certain capacity for such acts, but it will be at the price of perversion. Unlike bowlegs, sexual deformity harms others, as well as the original victim.[11]

These realistic comments run counter to the increasing propaganda by such organizations as NAMBLA (North American Man-Boy Love Association) and the Rene Guyon Society, groups which promote sexual activity between adults and children. It is a symptom of the corruption of our times that a "society" or an "association" should be formed for the express purpose of promoting sexual activity by youngsters under age ten. In his book, Linedecker devotes a chapter ("Sex by Age Eight") to the Rene Guyon Society, the Childhood Sensuality Circle, the Paedophile Information Exchange (PIE) and NAMBLA.[12] The Guyon Society claims five thousand supporters and works for such goals as changing statutory rape laws to permit parents to allow sexual activity by their youngsters before the age of eight. The Childhood Sensuality Circle has fashioned "A Child's Sexual Bill of Rights," which includes the "rights" to learn lovemaking as soon as he or she is able to understand. . .the "right" to sexual relationships with parents, siblings, or other adults and children. . .the "right" to explore one's own body without any kind of direct or indirect adult interference.

In 1978 the North American Man-Boy Love Association was formed in Boston to promote pedophilia as a lifestyle, to defend men accused of sex crimes with boys, and to lobby against age-of-consent laws. PIE was formed in Scotland in 1974, with the same thrust as the other organizations just mentioned. Like the others, it claims that pedophilia is normal and it seeks to build a sense of community among pedophiles.

The facts are that sexual activities by children have devastating—and lasting—harmful effects on the children involved. Psychologists are virtually unanimous on this point. For instance, a study of the use of children in pornography, funded by the National Center on Child Abuse and Neglect, concluded that:

> The data strongly support the child remembering feeling anxious and fearful at the time of the [sexual] experience and angry at the event on follow-up. Children had vivid imagery of the event, frequent flashbacks and memory of the court/legal process. Also there was a high percentage (over 50%) of intrusive thought symptomology and avoidance behavior.
>
> The data support suggesting that the psychological trauma experienced by the child is expressed as post-traumatic stress disorder, chronic type. There is also data to support that child pornography is related to other social

problems such as substance abuse when alcohol and/or drugs were used as the lure by the pedophile or producer of the pornography. More notable in the child population, however, was the behavior of dropping out of high school. . . .[13]

Children who pose for pictures begin to think of themselves as objects to be sold; they choke off their feelings of affection and finally respond like objects rather than people:

Further, authorities generally agree that the deep psychological and humiliating impact of such sexual activity perpetuates a vicious cycle whereby the degraded child joins other deviant populations: drug addicts, prostitutes, criminals, and pre-adult parents. More tragic, however, is the fact that sexually exploited children tend to become sexual exploiters of children themselves as adults.[14]

In a friend of the court brief in the U.S. Supreme Court case of *New York* v. *Paul Ira Ferber*, Covenant House cited numerous authorities for the position that "kiddie porn" is "highly destructive to children," "devastating," and likely to produce "psychic trauma" and "[m]assive acute anxiety" for children involved.[15] The fear of exposure dogs the child's heels for the rest of his life, as he or she vainly struggles with perpetual insecurity due to fear of later public exposure and ridicule. But these psychological burdens may pale beside the immediate trauma of venereal disease and the growing likelihood of infectious—and incurable—AIDS caused by some kinds of promiscuous sexual activity.

Sexual Health for Children

Many psychologists now question whether grammar school children should deal with sex at all. They have come to understand the importance of the integrity of the "latency period."

This is the time of life when the child normally renounces what Freud called his "oedipal strivings" and represses from conscious memory his early experiences of childhood longing and attraction to the parent of the opposite sex. Dr. Rhonda L. Lorand, a clinical psychoanalyst and author of the bestselling book *Sex and the Teenager* has written that with the onset of the latency period the child quiets down and turns his attention to achievements which lead him into the grownup world. The sexual passions and interests are channeled into learning concrete subjects, skills and hobbies. The learning process, Freud discovered, works with the sublimated sexual curiosity, sublimated sexual energy, and the sublimated aggressive instinct.[16]

The latency period is extremely important for proper psychological development, as psychiatrist Dr. Melvin Anchell points out:

> The natural re-direction of the sexual energies is manifested in the intense capacity and desire for learning characteristic of this period of transition between childhood and adolescence. Usually occurring between the ages of six and thirteen, it is known as the "latency period," because the sexual drive per se remains dormant and latent. School children of this age are generally indifferent or asexual in their attitude toward their peers of the opposite sex. They are inherently preoccupied with their own individual aims. Subconscious sexual urges are released in fantasies and dreams.[17]

These psychological insights help explain why children under age thirteen should not even *see* pornography. For obvious reasons, they should not *do* pornography. Forcing a child into sexual experience before he is ready is like forcing him to walk before he can even stand erect. On the journey from infancy to adulthood, there are natural progressive stages of sensual awareness. To "jump" past an essential stage of psychic development is as traumatic for a child as being thrown into combat would be for a civilian who never went through boot camp.

This last analogy understates the problem. The civilian might survive combat because he is, presumably, an adult with formed character, developed muscles, and an agile mind. But the ten-year-old thrust into the world of pornography, forced or tricked into posing for a sado-masochistic film where he or she is worked over by an oversexed aggressor, has no psychic resources to cope with the situation. Scarcely beyond the age when he took a teddy bear to bed at night, the child must fake an ecstasy without romance, without affection, without love. An adult risks psychosis when forced to perform on schedule, night after night, with strangers whose perversions he or she senses. For the ten-year-old such a life does not *risk* self-destruction; it *is* self-destruction.

Child pornography is the worst form of child abuse. It infects the child's body. It twists the child's attitudes toward love, sex, and fatherhood. For the father-figure pornographer who handles him for a moment's stolen pleasure engenders in him a deep and abiding hatred.

Child Pornography and the Law

The State of New York and nineteen other states[18] have attempted to deal with the child pornography problem by prohibiting the distribution of material which depicts children engaged in sexual conduct without requiring that the material be legally "obscene." One Paul Ira Ferber, the owner of a Manhattan bookstore specializing in "sexually oriented products," a euphemism much like calling a rattlesnake "lethally oriented," was convicted under New York State law for selling two films devoted almost exclusively to showing young boys masturbating. The law provides:

> A person is guilty of promoting a sexual performance by a child when, knowing the character and content thereof, he produces, directs or promotes any performance which

includes sexual conduct by a child less than sixteen years of age.

Among its definitions, the statute included these:

"Sexual conduct" means actual or simulated sexual intercourse, deviate sexual intercourse, sexual bestiality, masturbation, sado-masochistic abuse, or lewd exhibition of the gentials.

The point of this law was to proscribe commercialized depictions of children in sexual activity even if that activity was not technically "obscene" by the complicated 1973 *Miller* v. *California* definition. In *Miller*, the Supreme Court limited the law's reach to "hard-core" pornography only. The Court's definition of "hard core" concentrated on "the dominant theme of the material taken as a whole" and included the patent offensiveness of the depiction when measured by "contemporary community standards." This definition did not help curb child pornography. It may be useful in dealing with marginal "art" and in striking a social balance between community puritanism and perversity, but the Court's definition assumes that the "actors" in the film or photo are consenting adults who know what they are getting into. It does not address the problem of serious and lasting harm to a ten-year-old whose momentary act may *not* fit the "dominant" theme or be *patently* offensive, but is nonetheless irreparably traumatic to the child.

The New York Court of Appeals overturned the state law. It agreed with Ferber that the First Amendment of the Constitution precludes a state from prohibiting promotion of a child's sexual performance unless that performance is technically obscene.

The appeals court thus disregarded the Legislature's finding at the time it passed the law:

The legislature finds that there has been a proliferation of exploitation of children as subjects in sexual performances. The care of children is a sacred trust and should not be abused by those who seek to profit through a commercial network based upon the exploitation of children. The public policy of the state demands the protection of children from exploitation through sexual performances.

In an antiseptic opinion that treated the filming of children in sex acts as little different from depicting them in any other activity, and suggesting that the legislature's concern was at root only a matter of subjective taste, the appeals court overturned the law. The statute, it said

discriminates against films and other visual portrayals of non-obscene adolescent sex, solely on the basis of their content, and since no justification has been shown for this distinction other than special legislative distaste for this type of portrayal, the statute cannot be sustained.[19]

Fortunately for the children of America, the U.S. Supreme Court showed greater realism. The Court opened by holding that a State has more freedom to proscribe works which depict children in sexual acts or lewd exhibitions. For the State's interest in "safeguarding the physical and psychological well being of a minor" is "compelling." The prevention of sexual exploitation and abuse of children constitutes a government objective of surpassing importance.

Further, the *Miller* standard of obscenity "bears no connection to the issue of whether a child has been physically or psychologically harmed in the production of the work." The court added that the First Amendment value of permitting photographic reproductions of children engaged in lewd sexual conduct is exceedingly modest if not *de minimis* (i.e., trivial).

The Supreme Court adjusted its general formula defining obscenity in the following respects: the jury "need not find that the material appeals to the prurient interest of the average person; it is not required that sexual conduct portrayed be done so in a patently offensive manner; and the material at issue need not be considered as a whole." In effect, the Court carved out an exception—along with such long-standing ones as libel and "fighting words"—to the rule that "speech" may never be controlled by law.[20]

Predators Not Defeated

One battle a war does not make. The predatory hedonists lost *Ferber* v. *New York*.[21] But they still prowl the streets.

"Leo" spends his spare time "cruising" eastern seaboard cities looking for pubescent boys to sodomize.

Lollitots and *Chicken Brats* and countless other magazines that pander to a lust unspeakable in its evil still circulate in a thousand "bookstores" where "adults" escape from reality through fantasies no decent man would entertain.

NAMBLA circulates its newsletter and the Rene Guyon Society holds its clandestine meetings—and both keep promoting incest and pederasty as "acceptable lifestyles."

For convictions like Ferber's are few and far between—and when they are forthcoming, the punishment often is light and the deterrence, consequently, low.

So the predatory hedonists' war of attrition against our nation's children goes on. And the body-count is upwards of one million physically barely living, spiritually dead children.

The count will go up as more children are swallowed by the modern Moloch that is child pornography and child abuse, until the public at last demands tough laws, aggressive enforcement, and severe penalites.[22]

But after *Ferber*, the fault is not the Supreme Court's. It is ours. For as a society we seem unwilling to face up to the fact that even the founder of Christianity sometimes urged severity:

But whoso shall offend one of these little [children]. . .it were better for him that a millstone were hung about his neck, and that he were drowned in the depth of the sea.

(Mt 18:6)

EIGHT

Pornography and the Law

MANY PEOPLE DERIVE their moral standards from the law. They believe that what the law condemns is "wrong" and what the law permits is "right." Thus the law is an educator. Adolescents and many adults who lack well-defined moral values tend to equate morality with legality and immorality with illegality. When they are told something is wrong, they will reply, "What's wrong with it? It's not against the law."

Traditionally, in Anglo-American law "the police power" legitimately protects public "health, safety, welfare, and morals."[1] The criminal law does this in two ways. First, it discourages violent attack by one citizen on another (murder, robbery, arson, rape, etc.) by threat of punishment. Second, it discourages *non-violent victimization* of persons by expressing the community's judgment that some non-violent actions are wrong in themselves, that they destroy the moral fiber of the people, and erode that sense of civility and respect for other people essential for human society.

Recently some intellectuals have pushed to "decriminalize" what they call "victimless crimes."[2] These include pornography, alcoholism, homosexual actions, gambling, and narcotics use. They say that the law should simply prohibit *violent* attacks on citizens and prevent children and non-consenting adults from being drawn into "victimless" crimes.

The "decriminalizers" attempt a radical separation between law's two functions. In essence, they say that the law may punish violent victimization but not non-violent victimization. Their attitude seems to be that people will be better if the law does nothing to give a more humane tone to society. They are in favor of public morality. But they naively think that people will be more moral if the law does nothing to protect public morality.

This was not the American view for the first 150 years of our history.

The Law and Public Morality

Control of obscenity has historically been the province of what we call "common law." Common law is different from "code law," the statutes and rules like those all taxpayers wade through with around April 15 every year. The history of American and British law has been the history of the common law. This is a process of case-by-case adjudication by individual judges through the generations, decisions guided by common sense, the ethical instincts and religious understandings of their times, and especially precedents from prior cases with similar facts.

The earliest obscenity case in the United States took place in 1815 in Philadelphia.[3] At the time there were no obscenity statutes on the books; the case was a common-law action. One Jesse Sharpless was convicted of exhibiting, for money, a painting "of a man in an obscene, impudent, and indecent posture with a woman." In 1821, a Peter Holmes published the book *Memoirs of a Woman of Pleasure*, or *Fanny Hill*, in Massachusetts, and was convicted in a common-law prosecution.

In 1821, Vermont, followed by Connecticut and Massachusetts within fifteen years, adopted the first state laws against indecent literature. In 1842 the United States Congress adopted section twenty-eight of the customs law, which prohibited importing indecent and obscene pictorial art. In 1865 a Congress preoccupied by the Civil War made it a criminal offense to send obscene literature through the U.S. mails. In 1873 the Comstock Act passed both Houses of Congress after less than an hour of debate. It provided for a fine up to $5,000—then an enormous sum in terms of real purchasing power—and up to *five years* in prison for the first offense, double for second offenders, for sending pornography through the mails.

This capsule history is quite significant. "Code law" is the response of legislatures when common law cannot deal with new situations. Criminal code law, by imposing penalties with clearly escalating levels of severity, expresses the community's moral outrage about certain conduct. The criminal code is more than a list of negative prohibitions and punishments. It is also an expression of the community's moral standards, a way for the leaders of the community to educate everyone about what conduct is "good" and "bad." For this reason, even laws which are ineffectively or indifferently enforced— such as those laws against shoplifting and jaywalking—play an important part in the protection of community standards.[4]

Thus, for the last century, Americans took for granted that the country had public standards (however bawdy its frontier towns), that law should protect these standards, and that obscenity was a serious matter. Also, the actions of Congress indicate that it thought that the constitution's protection of "freedom of speech" had nothing to do with protecting obscenity.

The U.S. Supreme Court first reviewed the Comstock Act in 1896. A certain Lew Rosen, a New York publisher of a paper called *Broadway*, had been convicted of printing pictures of "females in different attitudes of indecency." The Supreme Court had to define obscenity. The trial judge in Rosen's conviction had formulated the "Hicklin rule," derived from a 1868 English common law case *Regina* vs. *Hicklin*. This case had defined obscenity as material "with a tendency to deprave and corrupt those whose minds are open to such immoral influences." The Supreme Court agreed.[5]

But this definition contained the seeds of its own rejection.

It implied that "harm" did occur and that it was discernable, a view many moderns were later to contest. More seriously, it measured obscenity by its possible impact on the *most susceptible* rather than on normal or mature persons. Critics of the Hicklin rule said it restricted serious literature and art. In a much later case Justice Frankfurter criticized the rule as "burning down the house to roast the pig."[6] He meant that it would prevent the people from reading literature harmless to the majority because it was possibly harmful to a small minority.

The Modern Approach: The Roth *Case*

This was a rule certain to be challenged in the Supreme Court. It was, but the Court held that it was still right to roast the pig while preserving the house. In two 1957 cases, *Roth* v. *United States* and *Alberts* v. *California,* the Supreme Court upheld, respectively, a federal statute making it illegal to mail "obscene, lewd, lascivious, or filthy" materials or "other publications of an indecent character"; and a California law banning the publication, advertising, sale, or distribution of "any obscene or indecent" material.[7] The Supreme Court's opinion boils down to two basic points. First, obscenity is not a form of expression which the First Amendment to the Constitution protects. Second, the rule measuring what is obscene is no longer the Hicklin "impact-on-most-susceptible" rule, but rather a new definitional standard. Material is legally obscene if

> to the average person, applying contemporary community standards, the dominant theme of the material taken as a whole appeals to prurient interest.

Prurient interest was defined as a "shameful or morbid interest in nudity, sex or excretion which goes substantially beyond customary limits of candor in description or representation."

In passing, the majority opinion noted that obscenity has

always been considered to be "without redeeming social importance."

Courts and legislatures took their cue from the *Roth-Alberts* cases and widely adopted the Supreme Court's obscenity definition. For example, the New York State Legislature inserted the following into its penal code, a definition which became virtually universal:

> Any material or performance is "obscene" if a) considered as a whole, its predominant appeal is to prurient, shameful or morbid interest in nudity, sex, excretion, sadism or masochism and b) it goes substantially beyond customary limits of candor in describing or representing such matters, and c) it is utterly without redeeming social value. Predominant appeal shall be judged with reference to ordinary adults unless it appears from the character of the material or the circumstances of its dissemination to be designed for children or other susceptible audience.

The first two standards are useful enough: they strike a reasonable balance, if you will, between prudity and nudity. They permit a literary work to contain an occasional off-color passage incidental to the development of character and plot. They recognize the merit is not burning down the house to roast the pig. They preserve community standards by upholding and indeed utilizing "customary limits of candor"—the custom has to be that of the community, which in turn is represented by the jury hearing the case.

However, the third standard—"utterly without redeeming social value"—opened a bottomless can of worms. This was not quite what the Supreme Court had said; though it had alluded to this point in *Roth*, what the Court *meant* was that *if* a thing is "obscene," it *follows* that it lacks redeeming social value, that is, the absence of "redeeming social value" is a consequent of a thing first being found "obscene."

Later the Supreme Court engrafted the New York language into its own definition of obscenity.[8] The result was to make the "redeeming social value" criteria *antecedent* to the finding of obscenity. That is, in order to find something obscene, one had to prove that it "utterly lacked redeeming social value"— along with dominant appeal, prurience, offense to customary limits of candor, and the other criteria for obscenity. This led to the unseemly—if not hypocritical—appearance of "literature experts" and "art critics" testifying with a straight face as "expert witnesses" that orgies on film "tell us something about what people are interested in" and thus have "redeeming social value."[9]

The Proper Limits of Courts

Nonetheless, the legal definition of obscenity is not unreasonable. The real problem in obtaining obscenity convictions lies elsewhere—in the propensity of courts, especially the Supreme Court, to construe "obscenity" as a "question of law" rather than a "question of fact."

Without becoming overly technical, we can explain the distinction simply: the jury decides the facts; judges declare the law. Juries deal with concrete events; judges with abstract propositions. Juries use common sense and personal experience, intuition, and even "gut feeling" to decide whether something actually happened or whether a course of conduct was "reasonable." Judges are bound by rules of evidence, presumptions, permissible inferences, and other abstractions. Juries are theoretically bound by the judge's definitions of the rules of law, which he reads to them just before they retire to the jury room to deliberate; but in practice they have wide latitude to follow their own instincts.

An obscenity trial in Virginia which I sat in on in 1980 shows how the jury system is supposed to work. The defendants were charged with six felony counts, one each for showing, for a price, in an "adult book store," five-minute movies of masturbation and sexual intercourse in vivid zoom-lens color close-ups. The three defense counsel brought in an expert witness from a local university, a "professor of human sexuality," who testified that "There is nothing prurient—morbid and excessive—in such actions."

Despite the learned abstractions of the professor, the members of the jury applied their common sense and quite sensibly found the defendants guilty. They may have realized that the professor's statement that there is nothing prurient about what was shown on the films subtly distorted the issue. The issue was not the actions on film, but the filming of what normal people consider very private activities, and especially the selling of those films to members of the public to entertain themselves by repeated viewing. The point was not whether the filmed actions in themselves are prurient or not, but whether the "dominant theme of the material taken as a whole" did appeal to *other people's* prurient interest.

Exercising its common sense, the jury was able to identify and punish obscenity. When a judge in a jury trial steps into the jury's shoes and begins to make himself the "trier of fact" instead of the articulator of the law, he walks where he should not go. The whole purpose of the criminal jury system is to apply the common sense of the community to the case at hand. Judges do not normally have the proper mindset to take on this role—a fact recognized by the universal rule that lawyers (whose ranks provide us our judges) cannot serve as members of a jury. While our system does provide for a "bench trial"— trial by judge alone—the defendant, or either party in a civil suit, can always request a jury trial. Experience teaches conclusively the "bench trials" work best when the issues are highly technical and legalistic, such as in anti-trust or bankruptcy matters. Juries are best when the issues include intuitive common-sense questions, such as what are the "contemporary community standards" for obscenity. After all, the jury is "the community."

Appellate courts function at another judicial level. These are groups of three, seven, or nine judges who hear appeals of cases decided at a lower level. The Supreme Court is the highest and last appellate court. Appeals deal almost exclusively with whether the trial judge properly applied the law when the original fact-finding trial took place in his court. The only time an appellate court can reverse a jury's finding of fact is in the rare situation where the jury held "contrary to the *manifest* weight of the evidence." This means that no reasonable person could have done what the jury did. The jury, because of bias, misleading comments by one of the attorneys, or for some other reason, disregarded the actual evidence and "found" what reasonable people would have to admit was pure fiction.

The appellate judges review the record of the trial, read long written essays called "briefs" submitted by attorneys for both sides, and hear short oral arguments by the lawyers. The appellate court judges then retire to their conference room and discuss the case. If they agree that "error" existed in the trial judge's use of the law or if the jury decided contrary to the manifest weight of the evidence—then they usually "reverse" and order a new trial.

Most of the questions raised on obscenity trials are questions of fact. It is a question of *fact* whether "to the average person" a film or magazine display has a "dominant" theme which taken as a whole appeals to prurient interest. Establishing "contemporary community standards" is solely a question of *fact*. The current "customary limits of candor" is also a question of fact. And whether the depiction goes "substantially" or just slightly or not at all beyond those limits is equally a question of fact. Thus the "trier of the facts"—the jury—is the only one competent to answer these questions. It is simply not within the proper purview of an appellate court to answer them. Unless the appellate court finds that obscenity laws were improperly applied, or that a jury's finding of obscenity was against "the manifest weight of the evidence," it should leave the jury's findings of fact alone. If it does otherwise, the appellate court usurps the role and prerogative of the jury, constitutes itself as a trial court, and distorts the judicial process. An appellate court that rules on the facts of an obscenity trial is playing the role of an "ultimate board of censorship," not a court of law.

Yet this is just what the Supreme Court often did in the 1960s. It allowed itself to be persuaded that it, the Court, had to spend time reviewing the actual films, reading the actual books, that juries had already found—as a matter of fact—to be obscene. Not only was such conduct demeaning. Not only was it a waste of valuable judicial time. It was a distorting mixture of two quite separate roles and a rejection of the classic separation of tasks that had characterized American jurisprudence at least since the colonial trial of John Peter Zenger for criminal libel in New York in 1735.[10]

Emerging Confusions after Roth

In its 1957 *Roth* decision, the Supreme Court held that obscenity is not *protected* speech. That is, for constitutional purposes, obscenity—or pornography—is not "speech" at all. *Roth* also set forth a complicated but fairly balanced and potentially workable definition of obscenity for juries to apply to the facts in subsequent cases. This should have been the end of the matter.

But the pornographers did not give up after their defeat in 1957. They vastly increased their operations and more than matched those efforts with financial expenditures in the courtroom. In court, pornographers were helped by "civil libertarian" attorneys who uniformly if often unreflectively combine a secular humanist moral viewpoint (there are no moral absolutes) with a political theory that overstresses "freedom" (more often, license) as essential to the good society.

The American Civil Liberties Union promotes the theory that "freedom of speech" means that for practical purposes there can never be any governmentally imposed restraints on the "speaker."[11] This social *laissez-faire* assumes that one unit of "speech" is just as good as another; that no one can judge degrees of moral, rhetorical, aesthetic, or social worth among competing "expression." This is an astounding position coming from college teachers and lawyers and other "learned" professionals, who, one would presume, can and do tell the difference in value between a work by Shakespeare and one by Mickey Spillane.

The notion that one page of "expression" is just as good as any other sounds absurd, but it recurs with tiresome frequency in the debate over control of pornography. For instance, when Larry Flynt, the publisher of *Hustler* magazine, was fighting an obscenity prosecution, his defenders urged that censorship of his magazine would quickly lead to censorship of the Bible and bonfires to burn Shakespeare's plays. This claim suggested that Flynt's defenders, however much time they spent reading the Gospel of Hedonism according to Flynt, had not spent much time reading the Gospel of Jesus according to John.

The Supreme Court had a bad time with obscenity cases in the 1960s. First, the court could scarcely ever agree on a consistent rationale for substituting its own judgment for both trial and lower appellate courts. Second, the court replaced the *Roth-Alberts* stress on "contemporary community standards" with a "national" standard for obscenity. This proved virtually unworkable because it was still up to local juries to define obscenity. How could a local jury define obscenity according to national standards when history and the constitution make it plain that the purpose of using a jury is to give *the local community* influence in the outcome of criminal trials? Third, the notion of "national" standards began to fall apart. It became obvious that what the community in San Francisco can tolerate may well turn the stomach of the community in Des Moines. A "national" standard looked like a lowest-common-denominator standard—that is, no standard at all.[12]

In the latter part of the 1960s, the Supreme Court gave up the pretense of consistency. In *Redrup* v. *New York* (1967),[13] it began to reverse obscenity convictions in a procedure known as *per curiam*—that is, by the "court as a whole" and without written opinion. This meant that the court could reverse when at least five members of the court, applying their *separate* tests, thought something was not obscene. The Supreme Court actually had the arrogance to reverse thirty-one lower court convictions, at the cost of countless thousands of prosecutorial man-hours, without even giving a reason!

The record was not entirely bleak: the Court did manage to find it within itself to uphold protection of minors in *Ginsberg v. New York*.[14] It suggested, in *Redrup*, that the law could control instrusive thrusting of obscenity on non-consenting adults. It upheld, in *U.S. v. Reidel* [15] (1971), the power of Congress to proscribe distribution of obscene materials through the mails. But these cases were small oases of common sense in a desert of philosophical confusion.

The Supreme Court's Miller *Definition*

In 1973 in the case of *Miller* v. *California*[16] the U.S. Supreme Court attempted—successfully, I believe—to dispel the confusion. It undertook to redefine the "obscene," which by now it was ready to call "hard-core pornography." It rephrased *Roth* to define obscenity as material with the following three elements:

a) whether the average person, applying contemporary community standards would find that the work, taken as a whole, appeals to the prurient interest . . .

b) whether the work depicts or describes, in a patently offensive way, sexual conduct specifically defined by the applicable state law, and

c) whether the work, taken as a whole, lacks serious literary, artistic, political, or scientific value.

To leave no doubt as to what it had in mind, the Court gave two examples of what guideline b) means: "patently offensive represensations or descriptions of ultimate sexual acts, normal or perverted, actual or simulated: and . . . of masturbation, excretory functions, and lewd exhibition of the genitals."

Miller and a companion case clarified other matters as well.[17] First, the court made it clear that "community standards" are *not* national; it left the jury free to define "community," which now can be the town, city, county, or even the state. Thus the "community" will be reflective of the kind of people the obscene material is reaching. Second, the court stated that the only prosecutions permitted were of "hard core" pornography, thus protecting "soft core" pornography. Third, the court jettisoned the useless "utterly-without-redeeming-social-value" standard, thereby tossing out as well the hypocrisy of "expert witnesses" discovering "value" in utter filth. The definition is thus in many ways a marked improvement over the phraseology that had so bedeviled the Court over the prior twenty-five years.

Many who support legal controls over pornography were relieved that the court permitted protection of a modicum of public morality. Yet the Court has changed its mind about pornography many times and could well do so again as personnel on the Court changes. *Miller* was decided by a 5-4 vote. The four person minority was led by Mr. Justice Brennan, who believes that no one can produce a definition of obscenity that is not "void for vagueness," a criticism leveled at criminal laws that do not put prospective defendants on fair notice as to what conduct is prohibited. Consequently, there is little assurance that the Supreme Court jurists will permit American communities *any* legal protection of public morality in future years.

The Presidential Commission on Obscenity and Pornography

In the late 1960s, concerned about the growing problem of pornography and prodded by the writings and speeches of Attorney Charles H. Keating, Jr., founder of Citizens for Decency through Law, the Congress established a Presidential Commission to study the question and recommend stronger laws to control smut. But by one of those profound ironies that could not be mere accident, the Chairman and the majority of the Commission did the opposite. They urged the "decriminalization" of adult pornography and expressed their doubts about the utility of efforts to insulate children from pornography.[18]

One naturally asks how this could happen. How can otherwise intelligent people think that society is unharmed by "entertainments" which glorify the exploitation of women by men, reduce sex to the momentary couplings of barnyard animals in heat, and which operate as how-to-do-it manuals for criminal assault and statutory rape? The United States Senate must have wondered too because it voted by the lopsided margin of 60-5 to reject the majority report and, in effect, to adopt the report of an outraged minority.

The answer, though complicated, is worthy of attention, for the Presidential Commission majority report, which purported to find that "pornography causes no harm," still receives good press.

The Presidential Commission reached naive conclusions largely because it used a suspect methodology to study pornography.[19] For example, the research staff presumed that "harm" from pornography had to be direct, immediate, and measurable. It denied the reality of attitude changes, moral decline, or long-range debasement of values, all of which common sense tells us do in fact flow from unrestrained immersion in pornographic fantasy.

One experiment, typical of the Commission's approach, was to have a group of college students view porn films for hours at a time and then attempt to measure the extent of their physical arousal. Not surprisingly, after initial titillation, the students became sated. Noting that the students' sexual excitement declined, the "researchers" concluded that pornography has no lasting impact.

The Commission's researchers made so many mistakes that their errors defy easy summary. Suffice it to say that this approach asks the wrong question in the wrong way and thus produces the wrong answer.

Three Commission members, Rev. Morton Hill, Rev. Winfrey Link, and Charles H. Keating, Jr., vigorously contested the "findings" of the majority. The two clerics demonstrated the slipshodness of the methodology and said that the Commission staff had been unwilling to cooperate with committee members who did not share the majority's presuppositions.

Commissioner Keating went further. He thought it necessary, in what surely must have been an unprecedented step, to file a lawsuit against the Commission chairman in order to obtain access to certain Commission documents and to gain adequate time to compose a rebuttal to the majority report.[20]

Keating's minority report pointed out that the Commission had divided itself into four subcommittees which met infrequently, held no public hearings in major cities, and delegated most of the work to staff. Keating pointed out that the Commission had largely ignored the enabling legislation establishing the Commission that directed it to include people "from organizations and professions who have special and practical competence or experience with respect to obscenity laws." Keating wanted the Commission to look at actual police cases where immersion in pornography immediately preceded commision of a sex crime. He summarized twenty-six actual cases from around the country, including pornography-related assaults, rapes, sex perversion, child molestation, and even murder. But the Commission rejected his suggestion and continued its policy of relying on sociologists and clinical researchers rather than police officers, vice squad detectives, and juvenile case workers.

The Commission's methodology was to develop, through contract and staff work, a series of "Technical Reports." These were to be the basis for subcommittee reports which eventually were to lead to the Commission Panel Reports, and these in turn were to be the basis of the Commission Overview Report. In practice, however, the Commission reversed this order; later reports were completed before the reports on which they were supposedly based were finished. As Keating stated in his dissenting report:

> As a matter of fact, the Final Draft of the Overview Report was completed prior to the final drafts of the four

Panel Reports upon which it was supposed to rest, and the four Panel Reports, which were supposed to rest upon the Technical Reports, were completed before the completion of the Technical Reports. Improbable as it seems, the Technical Reports continued to be edited by the Staff, after the last full meeting of the Commission. . . .

The majority report and the underlying panel and technical reports took a tolerant view toward pornography. They claimed that there was no evidence that pornography causes harm, that there appeared to be little money made by the porno industry, that pornography resembled "sex education," that pornography filled a need by making helpful sexual material available to people, and that all laws controlling pornography directed at adults should be repealed.

It is little wonder that the Senate voted 60-5 to reject the majority report. The same month as that Report was made public, the Senate voted 79-0 to pass a bill that would sharply curtail the amount of obscene advertising that pours into American homes through the mail.

The Proposed Revised Federal Criminal Code

For many years the Congress has worked on revising the Federal Criminal Code but, as of spring of 1984, had not yet passed a final version. Although the principal purpose of the revision is to gather together and systematize scattered sections of the law, proposed versions have contained controversial changes in substantive law. Some of these changes affect the control of pornography.

The importance of these changes cannot be overstated. The federal prosecutors are the last line of defense against the smut peddlers. They have the resources and competence necessary to take on big-time pornographers, and through the F.B.I., they can conduct interstate investigations. By contrast, many local city or county prosecutors are relative amateurs. They lack experience, staff, and investigative resources to trace the twisting channels by which a pornographic film traveled from filming in California to advertising in Chicago to, say, showing in Indiana.

Federal prosecutors can bring only those cases warranted under the law. They will be weak if the law is weak, and the laws about pornography in the proposed revision need strengthening.

In 1980 Congress came close to passing the revision. The Senate and the House of Representatives considered two different bills. The House bill dealt with pornography only under the rubric, "Sexual Exploitation of Children." That is, it proposed to do *nothing* to prevent adult pornography. Moreover, the bill proposed *nothing* to prevent depictions of *adult* pornography from *reaching* children. This was basically a rehash of the Presidential Commission's decriminalization proposals which Congress had rejected out of hand a decade earlier.

The House bill's laws against "sexual exploitation" of minors were weak for many reasons. First, the proposed penalty was a maximum fine of $10,000, even though the penalty for distributing adulterated eggs would be $25,000 and, under certain conditions, $50,000 for violating noise emission standards. The proposed bill thus says that is at least two and a half times more evil to sell adulterated eggs than it is to sell children's videotaped adultery and it is five times more evil to sell a power mower that is too noisy than to sell children into sexual bondage to entertain the perverted lust of pedophiles.

The Senate bill had other problems.

First, it defined "minor" to exclude youngsters aged sixteen to eighteen. This self-limitation is unnecessary. The term "minor" should mean any person under the age of eighteen years. Otherwise the federal prosecutors will be able to do nothing for example, if a nationwide Mafia-controlled porn syndicate produces cheap video cassettes of seventeen-year-olds (or twenty-seven-year-olds for that matter) committing sodomy, and sells them to children in bookstores across the street from the local public school.

Second, it adopted unnecessarily harsh standards of proof

for determining the age of minors "acting" in pornographic films. The Justice Department testified in 1978 that these standards will preclude successful prosecution in many cases.

Third, it proposed sanctions so ineffective as to make the law a virtual dead letter. Though $10,000 and ten years in jail *sounds* tough, there is no minimum penalty for convicted pornographers. In the real world the maximum is rarely given. The proposed sentencing section would have most sentences run concurrently. In short, the penalties would make it easy for the pornography kingpins to push some henchman up front to "take a fall" while the people high up in the chain of command are not even identified.

Obviously, if Congress is serious about curbing pornography, it must put some teeth into federal law. It must a) raise the age of a "minor" to eighteen; b) impose tough sanctions, including life imprisonment in the egregious case; and c) introduce a realistic definition of the crime, which would require only that the prosecutor prove the child in the film or photo *appeared* to be a minor. This is a judgment a jury can make *from the pictures themselves*, without requiring the prosecution to find the child, whose real name and whereabouts no one may know, or want to admit. Only then will there be a chance of preventing the use of children in films depicting bestiality and oral-genital sexual intercourse and gang orgies.

Another Senate bill proposing to revise the criminal code was seriously flawed in its provisions dealing with the dissemination of obscene material. For one thing, it failed to adopt by reference the general law of the existing statutes—a matter of including a simple statement that the legislative intent of the bill was not to replace existing law, but to incorporate it.

But the bill had other problems. It defined an offense as disseminating obscene material to any person *"in a manner affording no immediate effective opportunity to avoid exposure to such material."* This section would put the burden on the prosecutor to prove that a citizen could not "dodge out of the way" of oncoming pornography. Such a subjective standard would open a Pandora's Box of problems for the prosecution. Every key word—"immediate," "effective," "exposure"—would be subject to tortured judicial interpretation. Worst of all, the proposed section erodes the moral force of the law. It would focus on the question of whether some people were exposed to *some* pornography against their will and would neglect the *objective* evil of all pornography, regardless of whether a citizen wanted to see it or not.

The draft of this Senate bill also inexplicably defined "minor" as "an unmarried person less than seventeen years old." Another section of the same bill, one on "Conducting a Prostitution Business," more sensibly defined "minor" as "a person less than eighteen years old." Why was there this inconsistency in a Code designed to simplify and put order into the old law? The marital status of an individual is irrelevant to a bill penalizing exploitation of a minor in pornography. Such a requirement adds one more unnecessary burden to the prosecution. (It is not beyond the pale of possibility that the defense counsel will introduce evidence that the youngster was indeed married, perhaps even to the consort "acting" in the film!)

The bill also offered a seriously flawed definition of obscenity. For it stated, among other things, that material is obscene if, taken as a whole, "it appeals predominantly to the prurient interest of—1) the average person . . . " But in *Miller* the Supreme Court gave a different definition:

> Whether the average person, applying contemporary community standards would find that the work, taken as a whole, appeals to the prurient interest . . . "

The distinction may seem innocuous to non-lawyers, but in law every word counts. The Senate bill, in fact, has a loophole big enough to drive a truck-load of pornography through.

Under the bill's definition, a defense counsel for an accused pornographer could claim that the material in a given trial is *so* offensive and disgusting that it does not appeal to the prurient interest *of the average person*. In other words, according to this Alice-in-Wonderland reasoning, the jury could be forced to decide that the depictions are so *factually* obscene that it could not find it *legally* obscene! A pornographer in Cleveland was once acquitted under such a mistaken definition.

There are other weaknesses; but prolonged legalistic analysis of specifics can distract from the essential point: it is possible, under the guise of a "revision" and "codification" of the federal obscenity law, for Congress so to weaken the law that its deterrent value evaporates. Under the pretense of "doing more" about the growing pornography plague, Congress could render the law so feeble that the district attorneys end up doing less—or nothing at all.[21]

NINE

What You Can Do

W HERE IS OUR ANGER?
Have we lost our capacity for outrage? Are we, as a people, so jaded by the quantity of filth around us that we are paralyzed? Or do we think it does not matter, as long as—somehow—our own children don't get involved in it?

Pornography exploits. It exploits women; and it exploits children and young adults of both sexes.

Worse, pornography *teaches* exploitation. It is "sexist" to the core: it glorifies male fantasies of dominating women. It is anti-child: it glorifies actions which amount to no more than raw child-abuse. It uses and abuses women and children in its portrayals. And these portrayals amount to nothing more than how-to-do-it manuals, teaching the same neuroses to their readers and viewers as the manufacturers of the portrayals themselves suffer. Pornography is a plague that destroys mental health.[1] Those who promote it are carriers of a plague.

We cannot be indifferent to this moral pollution.

There are about 5,000 MacDonald's fast-food restaurants in the United States. There are about 15,000 "adult" bookstores in the United States. One can scarcely drive through any medium-size town or large city without seeing the golden arches of MacDonalds. But since there are *three times* as many porn shops, the odds are three times greater that as we drive along we will run into a pornographic store. Our teenage children and their friends are three times more likely to have the opportunity to watch an X-rated movie that to find a place to buy a "Big Mac."

Now if MacDonalds, which actually sells rather good food, were to use ingredients that infected their patrons with a strange malady that causes, in many cases, venereal disease, child abuse, sexual assault, or rape, would we not campaign to close MacDonalds down? Would we not insist they clean up their kitchens and change the stuff they put into their food? Would we not file nuisance actions, ask the police to comb the criminal code for statutory violations, demand that the "consumer protection" agencies "do something" to protect women and children from the plague this fast-food chain was spreading?

Of course we would. Then why do we allow young men to consume the moral pollution that spreads the disease of addiction to pornography?

If there were "adult narcotics-stores" scattered around every city, where people could go for a cheap chemical "fix," where the proprietors would pander to the patrons' addictions to different forms of drugs, would the authorities not take action? Why are they so supine, in many cases, in dealing with the "adult bookstores," where people go for a cheap psychological "fix," where proprietors pander to the patrons' addiction to different forms of sexual perversion?

The answer is simple: Prosecutors put pornography at low priority where there seems to be little public support for stronger efforts.

You and I must change their attitude. Beginning with child pornography, a crime so unspeakable—the destruction of innocence through perversion, for the sake of money—that one almost gags to talk about it, we must persuade the prosecutors to go on the offensive. And then all forms of pornography must be attacked—for in principle the stuff is the same: the exploitation of one human being, usually women, sometimes boys, by predatory hedonists who respect nothing but their own pursuit of pleasure. And who care neither that they may infect others with herpes, AIDS, syphilis, or gonorrhea, nor that they certainly will destroy the mental health of their victims.

But when we refuse to "get involved," community standards collapse, prosecutors turn their attention to other matters, the merchants of vice are emboldened. "All that is necessary for the triumph of evil is that good men do nothing." This saying, usually attributed to Edmund Burke, expresses one of the less pleasant truths about human nature.

This saying is true for two reasons. First, human nature has a self-destructive tendency, something like a spiritual "law of entropy." Without constant effort to maintain "good," a *devolution* will occur. Without strenuous exercise, athletes get flabby; without renovation, neighborhoods deteriorate into slums; without conscious striving to practice virtue, people begin to indulge in vice.

Second, evil will triumph unless we resist it because "evil" is an active and aggressive force in human affairs. Evil is like the barbarians pounding at the walls of ancient Rome: if the watchmen on the towers do nothing to repel the invader and to shore up the crumbling fortifications, then the attackers will break in and sack the city.

In both senses, the statement is true about pornography. To paraphrase: "All that is necessary for the triumph of pornographic immorality and the ultimate seduction of our society is that good men do nothing." The purpose of this chapter is to outline what is required to fight back.

Who Are the Good Men?

It is easy to say that the job is "somebody else's." In a sense, it is. The job of controlling pornography, of protecting the children, of discouraging exploitation of women, of limiting crime in the "combat zones" (which are often virtually the whole city)—this job surely belongs to the "good men" who are legislators, police, prosecutors, and judges.

For without strong laws, the police cannot act because the investigative cost is too great compared to the degree of anticipated deterrence. And without police who give top priority to this task, the prosecutors will not have evidence on which to base indictments. And without prosecutors who care about the children and their moral environment, their staff lawyers will not go forward aggressively to seek convictions. But even with all these, without judges who understand their duty to preserve the moral tone of society and to "protect the consumers" from corruption, there will be only slap-on-the-wrist penalties that make a mockery of public morality and leave the predatory hedonists free to prowl the streets again, looking for innocents to devour. "For want of a nail, the shoe was lost . . . "

But the job is not entirely "somebody else's." As a *Pogo* cartoon said, some years ago: "We have met the enemy, and they is *us*." More eloquently, as Cassius said to Marcus Brutus in Shakespeare's *Julius Caesar:* "The fault, dear Brutus, is not in our stars; it is in ourselves."

One good man who is doing something and is not blaming the stars is Richard Enrico of Fairfax County, Virginia, the most populous metropolitan Washington, D.C., suburb. This is an area of upward-mobile, well-educated, self-consciously sophisticated and frequently affluent people. Fairfax County is by no means a rock-ribbed fundamentalist town in the south. Nonetheless, Enrico, an Episcopalian layman, like St. George slaying the dragon, has driven some powerful sword-thrusts into the monster that is pornography—and he's done it on his own.

Here is a reprint of a newspaper columnist's summary of Mr. Enrico's efforts:

VIRGINIA MAN ENTHUSIASTIC
IN HIS WAR AGAINST PORNOGRAPHY

The most remarkable people I come across in writing this column are not the clergy—folks paid to be good. It's the people out in the pews who are inspired to serve the Lord.

Take Richard Enrico, who appears to be a quiet, middle-aged man with grey hair. He is an Episcopalian, with appropriate manners. But he has created a movement in Fairfax, Va., called Citizens Against Pornography, which already has:

Replaced a 48-foot billboard of Pia Zadora in a bikini advertising a movie about incest with one that ran over the Christmas season featuring these 10 words against a huge rainbow: "This Season Give Yourself JESUS— His Love Endures Forever."

Convinced the three biggest drug store chains in northern Virginia to stop selling Hustler magazine— permanently.

Persuaded George Mason University to cancel an X-rated film scheduled by students entitled "Debbie Does Dallas," and closed a video store selling it.

Gotten two department stores—the Hecht Co. and Montgomery Ward—to stop advertising "intimate" see-through lingerie.

All of these steps were achieved without any pickets or marches. Enrico, 51, is a management consultant who works quietly on the telephones and typewriter. But when he talks, it is with authority, righteous anger, and enthusiasm for how "God is using me."

In his talks—whether in the pulpit or before a Republican committee or Rotary Club, he gets people's attention quickly by quoting Hosea 4:6 "My people perish for lack of knowledge," adding, "Are you aware that 20 million Americans have herpes, according to the Communicable Disease Center in Atlanta? What does that have to do with pornography? Everything. It is because pornography is coming into homes on video cassettes, TV, movies, magazines, even commercials—that people are turning to lust and to sexual affairs.

"We are a nation with 'In God We Trust' on our coins, but law enforcement officials estimate that as many as 1 million youngsters (ranging from 16 to under a year) are sexually molested and then filmed or photographed. One magazine, Baby Sex, shows six-month old infants in sexual acts with adults!

"Nationwide, an estimated 50,000 children disappear a year. Many are into lives of sexual exploitation. The 25th anniversary edition of Playboy has a full-color cartoon of a woman being sexually ravaged by a dog and a cartoon of Santa Claus having sexual intercourse with one of the reindeer."

He then describes Hustler's recent issues, and hands out copies to clergy groups, saying "Some of you are so heavenly-minded you are no earthly good. You need to look at what is in these magazines!

"The August issue of 1983 had a picture of a male who looked like Jesus Christ, in the nude, lying beside a man and a woman in the nude. The January issue had a nude picture of the 'first lady' and the 'president' performing sodomy on another woman . . . Cardinal Cooke, who just died, was in hell with Madalyn Murray O'Hare throwing him a Bible."

"Larry Flynt, the man who publishes this magazine is in federal prison right now. So why is your local drugstore selling this stuff? This is ludicrous? Christians are going in and shopping in these stores, and not saying anything. Why not? Everywhere I go, the stores tell me I am the first to complain. Why? Why?"

Enrico quit his consulting business to spend full time on the issue, working for a year out of a small office in The Church of the Apostles, where his wife is a secretary. This has been financially difficult, for he is working "on faith" and depends on contributions.

But he has put together a list of 220 churches, 70 organizations or businesses and 3,500 people who support his work. The churches are of all denominations, which put aside traditional factionalism to fight a commonly perceived evil.

What is important is that they have found a strategy any community could adapt, a "plan so simple it defies imagination," says Enrico. "In its 1973 decision, the Supreme Court said it can't define pornography—that each community has to set its own standard. So I'm saying, let's define it as getting Playboy and Hustler out of the stores.

"If righteous people would do that, we can turn this nation around. United we stand and divided we fall."

Interestingly, the American Civil Liberties Union can see nothing illegal in what Enrico is doing. He is not acting with legal suits, but in arousing people to speak up to businesses who are more interested in consumer loyalty than in the sale of a particular product.

Joseph Pollar, vice president of Peoples Drug Stores, said Hustler was being taken out of Northern Virginia stores—not those in Washington or nearby Maryland, "in response to some local religious groups that asked us enough, that we did it." Rite-Aid Drug Stores, on the other hand, removed Hustler from all 1,147 stores nationally.

Enrico is inspiring others to fight. A big sign advertising chickens at a Holly Farms Store in Herndon came down within 24 hours when a woman objected to the slogan, "Try our bigger breasts."

His next porno target is "SUPER TV," which is supposed to be scrambled but which shows long sequences of homosexuality, group sex, etc. If Hustler is the definition of the community standard, clearly hard-core porn on TV is unacceptable.

What can you do? First, ask your pastor to preach on the subject, perhaps using the text Job 31:1—"I have made a covenant with my eyes not to look lustfully at a girl." Or Ephesians 5:11: "Have nothing to do with the fruitless deeds of darkness, but rather expose them."

Second, write Richard Enrico, Citizens Against Pornography, P.O. Box 6434, Falls Church, Va. 22046, for information, with a small contribution to cover his costs. Then be bold!

Most of us cannot undertake a one-man crusade. But we can help the individuals who do. And we can join and support those organizations founded by the "one man" who saw the problems clearly and had the courage to act.

I am aware of three organizations that have been especially effective. These are *Citizens for Decency through Law*, founded by Attorney Charles H. Keating, Jr., in the late 1950s; *Morality in Media*, founded by Rev. Morton A. Hill, in the early 1960s; and the *National Federation for Decency*, founded at the end of the 1970s by Rev. Donald Wildmon. In my judgment they are complementary. Each has had considerable impact; but in a David vs. Goliath fight, each needs greater membership, financial contributions, and publicity.

Citizens for Decency through Law, 2331 West Royal Palm Road, #105, Phoenix, Arizona 85021; phone (602) 995-2600. In 1957, the same year as the *Roth* decision, which held that obscenity is not constitutionally protected speech, a clergyman challenged a young Cincinnati attorney, Charles Keating, to put his Christian faith into action and "Do something" about the spread of obscene literature in such forms as pulp novels, "detective" stories, and "men's magazines." Keating formed a nonprofit, tax-deductible educational corporation called Citizens for Decent Literature, with the moderate purposes of a) educating the public to the state of the law and their rights to law enforcement against illegal actions such as pandering obscenity, and b) supporting prosecutors with able lawyers with greater experience in a field of litigation which, Keating correctly foresaw, could become the province of highly skilled defense-counsel technicians who would "outgun" the nonspecialist prosecutors.

With the transition from printed obscenity to photographed pornography in the 1960s, CDL adopted its present name. During that decade, while earning a living for his wife and six children and carrying on an energetic legal/business practice, Keating wrote powerful denunciations of the growing corruption and spoke widely around the country trying to awaken people to join the defense of basic public morality. For his pains he was the target of considerable personal abuse, occasional serious threats, and even vexation lawsuits designed to cripple him financially.

Citizens for Decency through Law is a membership organization which, like the others mentioned in this chapter, needs—and deserves—your support. CDL's approach is unique. It fights the war on the battlefield as well as the home front by sending attorneys into court on behalf of the laws upholding public decency. One cannot stress how important it is to have an experienced attorney prosecuting obscenity cases. The attorney must be experienced both as a general legal practioner and in this highly technical field of law. When a defense counsel earns, for one case, a fee as large as the prosecutor's salary for a year, the prosecutor is David and the defense counsel Goliath. By helping the prosecutors, CDL evens the odds.

Morality in Media, Inc., 475 Riverside Drive, New York, NY 10115, phone (212) 870-3210, is the result of the dedication of Rev. Morton Hill, who was acting under the same inspiration that moved Charles Keating. Hill was also a member of the Presidential Commission of Obscenity and Pornography. Indeed, Hill's own "Minority Report," co-authored with Minister Winifrey Link, was only slightly less blunt than Keating's in its condemnation of the theories and tactics of the commission majority. The Hill-Link Minority Report has influenced the Supreme Court into upholding some laws against pornography.

Father Hill's organization keeps careful track of obscenity cases taking place around the country and publishes a very useful periodic *Reporter*, written by a skilled attorney, Paul McGeady. This newsletter helps subscribing prosecutors to keep up with key cases that might help or hurt their own prosecutions.

Perhaps even more important has been Morality in Media's

early success in sensitizing the public to the collapse of public standards in television—our primary entertainment medium. They have local chapters in many parts of the country, as does CDL. Morality in Media has been successful, to some degree, in giving citizens a vehicle by which they can organize and affect local programming, and the content of cable TV.

One of MM's finest contributions to this struggle is an hourlong television documentary on the effects of pornography with Ephrem Zimbalist, Jr., as narrator and host. This professionally-produced TV special is a candid and powerful expose of what is happening to our young people through the "sex revolution" spawned by pornography. MM's members in local chapters could do us all a great service by working to get independent television stations in their own towns and cities to screen this film.

National Federation for Decency, P.O. Drawer 2440, Tupelo, Mississippi 38803, phone (601) 844-5036. Methodist minister Donald Wildmon started NFD a few years ago operating on a slightly different insight from CDL and MM. Again, like Charles Keating and Father Morton Hill, Rev. Wildmon was initially moved by the collapse of moral standards in the media. His special focus has been television.

NFD monitors countless soap operas, films, comedies, and specials, to keep accurate count of the scenes of violence, suggested sex, and profane language; and to attend to the innuendos and sub'iminal values (or disvalues) promoted by the stories. Basing its conclusions on empirical data, NFD argues that over the last decade there has been a steady increase in violence, "dirty words," and sex on television, along with a surprising upsurge in crude attacks on Christianity.

We are familiar enough with the television's casual murders, the nonchalant one-night sexual escapades, the gratuitous close-ups of half-covered female anatomy, the light-hearted acceptance of the so-called "homosexual lifestyle." Many of us, however, may not have noticed how quick television is, these days, to portray Catholic priests as spiritual hypocrites and Protestant ministers as money-grubbing con men—and to omit entirely from their story lines any characterization of a Christian in a favorable light. But some of the recent attacks have become almost venomous.

The unique approach of the National Federation of Decency lies in what it does about this corruption. It utilizes a legitimate tactic as American and as old as the labor union movement: the boycott.

People are free to watch TV or not, Reverend Wildmon points out. They are free to buy the advertiser's product or to reject it, he adds. And if they are angry at the corruption the advertiser is putting before their children's eyes on television, they can refuse to buy his product. And they can, most especially, write to the President or Chairman of the company which sponsors the offending program and tell him *why* they have decided to reject his product in favor of one made by his competitor.

This is the crux. Big companies often do not realize what they are sponsoring. Their advertising department, or an outside ad agency working under contract from them, simply "buys time" in certain slots and pays the price demanded by the network. The network, in turn, sets its price based on the "ratings." It is paid according to how many viewers it can deliver to an advertiser.

But of course the advertiser's message is surrounded by, and is part of, the larger message of the whole program. If that message is, in effect, an R-rated or X-rated movie, then the company's message is part of offensive lust and violence. Indeed, the advertiser pays for it.

So the advertiser cannot escape responsibility for the television programming he supports, any more than a manufacturer of aspirin could avoid his responsibility for poisoning consumers by using filthy containers for his aspirin. In a free society the consumer surely can exercise his right to vote in the marketplace of products and services just as he exercises his right to vote in the marketplace of political candidates.

Most companies, though by no means all, are concerned about the quality of the materials they put before our families to watch on television. When enough citizens call their attention to the corruption their advertising is spreading, they usually act to remove it. Some are actually grateful for the reminder.

The special virtue of Rev. Wildmon's approach is that it does not rely on the vagaries of law, on the skills of prosecutors, or on judges' commitment to public decency. NFD tells people what companies sponsor what programs. NFD's newsletter also frequently prints the offensive excerpts from program transcripts, thus providing the subscriber with the facts and arming him to act even if he missed the program. It also gives sample protest letters that subscribers can use to write to advertisers. NFD will provide the name and address of the chief executive officer of the company so subscribers can write to him easily. And, when a company stops sponsoring offensive material on television, NFD urges its members to write a letter of thanks to the CEO for his social conscience.

Where Are the Christians?

Every American citizen should be concerned about the spread of moral pollution and the seduction of our society. For, like Lake Erie absorbing toxic waste, there is a point beyond which the life-support system becomes saturated and nothing can survive. A time is coming when the moral environment of our society will become so saturated with toxins that no decent value, neither self-control nor respect for others, nor fidelity to spouse, nor premarital chastity, nor the innocence of little children, will survive.

But Christians, especially, should know better. And they should do better. But many, if not most, do nothing.

"Eternal rest grant onto them, O Lord," begins an invocation some Christian churches use in their funeral services. Yes, one merits rest after he has worked. He rests once he is dead. Not before.

I cannot recall the leaders of the "mainline" denominations, including the established urban Protestant communions and the Catholic Church, *ever* speaking out forcefully about the toxin of pornography. Certainly there has been no sustained effort. A pastor here, a bishop there, may have said something to his flock. Now and then a priest like Fr. Hill or a minister like Rev. Wildmon commit their full-time efforts to the thankless job of being Dutch Boy with finger in a dike behind which rise floods of spiritual sewage.

Yet if anything should move the clergy, this should be it. *No one* defends child pornography. Only a minority, and they with specious arguments ("freedom of speech" when they really mean "freedom to make a buck"), defends adult pornography. And the laws are on the books. This is no new campaign to "impose private morality" on others; it is a timeless effort to preserve a spark of decency in society by keeping clear before our eyes what is decent, and indecent; noble, and ignoble; proper, and perverse; moral and immoral. And in all of it the spiritual life of our children—and of ourselves—is at stake. The issue is made to order for the clergy: it is, unlike matters of military strategy and economic arrangements in Latin America or South Africa, a spiritual matter on which the Bible gives clear guidance.

Yet the clergy are, by and large, silent. One may conjecture why this is. It is the fact. They have made their peace with the world. The trendy media and the social ethos are libertarian; it is "old fashioned" to speak out against pornography.

Still, oddly enough, the anti-pornography issue is a perfect "ecumenical" matter. Too often, ecumenical activity consists of polishing complex doctrinal formulas in vague language so that all factions can agree on some statement that means all things to all and nothing specific to any one denomination. Why cannot different Christian churches cooperate, in faith and in charity, on social and political action designed to preserve the moral basis of our society? The "separatist" Baptist Jerry Falwell has invited Catholic layman Charles Keating to preach on the evils of pornography on television and to his Lynchburg, Virginia, congregation. Perhaps the "separatists" know more about ecumenical cooperation than the ecumenists.

But despite absence of serious and sustained leadership from many of their clergy, Christians of all denominations are citizens. They need not take passive clergymen as models for civic activity. We had better not, for it we wait for the clergy to lead the crusade to save the children, the children will be lost.

Christians are citizens. They should be *good* citizens. One is not a good citizen if he sits back, does nothing, and watches his society destroy itself. If the enemy is at the gates, one grabs a weapon and runs to defend his family. Today, with pornography, the enemy is not only "at" the gates; the pornographers are *within* the gates. And they are heading up the street on the way to your house.

While laymen like Richard Enrico and Charles Keating work tirelessly to stop the pollution of our moral environment, too many of the rest of us are sitting back in our pews. Asleep. Resting.

Yet how easy it would be for each parish and each congregation to set up a committee on Public Morality, or a chapter of Citizens for Decency through Law, or Morality in Media, or National Federation for Decency. If the average congregation has 300 people in it—and many have far more—is it too much to ask that thirty people read the literature, invite the speakers, compose letters to legislators and to corporate chief executives, circulate the materials of CDL and MM and NFD, speak in the schools, explain to the local rent-a-video-program store why "porn" should not be carried, sit in on obscenity trials, provide funding for the national offices of the three organizations leading the fight?

What will you do?

Cliché Arguments

Designed to Create Confusion around the Problem of Pornography, Obscenity Law and Cableporn

WHEN YOU BEGIN AN ORGANIZED effort against the traffic in pornography and Cableporn in your community, certain cliché arguments will be brought up to weaken your effort. You will hear them in private conversation, in public debate and frequently in the media. These arguments and answers should be studied and mastered so that the facts will be brought out.

Prepared by Morality in Media, Inc., 475 Riverside Drive, New York, NY 10115

Pornography and Obscenity Law

1. Pornography is harmless. A presidential commission report said so.

Answer:
a) The Majority Report of the Presidential Commission on Obscenity and Pornography was called a "scientific scandal" by many in the scientific community. It was rejected by the U.S. Senate by a vote of 60 to 5. The Hill-Link Minority Report of that Commission was read into the record in both Houses of Congress as a "responsible position on the issues." The Hill-Link Report cited numerous instances where evidence was suppressed when it went counter to the pre-determined "findings" of the majority report. The Hill-Link Report and the chapters by Dr. Victor B. Cline in "Where Do You Draw the Line?" expose the majority report for what it was. In addition, studies in the Hill-Link Report show linkages between

exposure to obscene material and sexual deviancy, promiscuity, affiliation with criminal groups and more. However, extremists who want obscenity laws repealed, as the majority report recommended, began a campaign in early 1977 to have the report resurrected and considered a reputable document.

b) The Supreme Court in *Paris Theatre* v. *Slaton* (June 1973) said: "The sum of experience, including that of the past two decades, affords an ample basis for legislatures to conclude that a sensitive, key relationship of human existence, central to family life, community welfare and the development of human personality, can be debased and distorted by crass commercial exploitation of sex."

2. You can't legislate morality.

Answer:

a) On its face this cliché is absurd, because every law legislates morality. Every law sets some standard for its citizens, and every citizen must ultimately make the moral decision to obey or disobey.

b) Private morals are private; public morals are the business of the entire community, and the officers empowered by the community to defend the welfare of the community against the willful minority. Commercial obscenity is public business. Obscenity laws are designed to safeguard public morality, not private morality.

3. Obscenity is in the eye of the beholder. What is obscene to you may not be obscene to me.

Answer:

This implies that obscenity is subjective. It is not. It is the description or depiction of specific sexual activity, the description or depiction of which is prohibited by law, to protect the common good. It is as objective as stealing or murder. This statement also denies the existence of evil.

4. I'd rather see people make love than make violence.

Answer:

There is no love in pornography. It is totally loveless, debasing women, children, and humanity in general. In addition, violence is inherent in pornography.

5. *War, poverty, hunger, violence are the real obscenities. Sex is not obscene.*

Answer:

a) The extension of the word *obscenity* to cover all kinds of social evils is a recent development in our language. It is a well-known technique to confuse and blunt the force of obscenity law.

b) Of course sex is not obscene. It is the design and creation of God. It is the debasing abuse of sex that is obscene. And, as in the past, so now all over the country, legislatures and the judiciary definitely specify certain abuses of sex as obscene.

6. *If you don't like porn films and books, you don't have to see them or buy them, but don't interfere with my right to see or buy them.*

Answer:

a) I don't see or buy pornography, but it pollutes the environment in which I am trying to raise my children. Society does not want it, and has enacted laws against it.

b) The United States Supreme Court has said that what you do in the privacy of your home is your own business, but your privacy right does not extend to the market-place. It is against the law for anyone to sell or exhibit obscenity to you.

7. *Well, the Supreme Court has said a lot of things, but it still can't define obscenity.*

Answer:

This statement is incorrect. The Supreme Court defined obscenity in June of 1973 to the satisfaction of the majority of the American people.

8. Freedom of expression is protected by the First Amendment.

Answer:

It most certainly is. But the Supreme Court has said, and always held, that obscenity is not protected by the First Amendment. It is not protected expression, any more than libel or slander are. Obscenity is *not* a First Amendment issue. It is a *crime,* and 90 percent of the traffic in hard core pornography in the country is controlled by *organized* crime.

9. Who are you to tell me what I can see or read? You are imposing your morality on me.

Answer:

a) Nobody can tell you what to see or to read, but the community can tell you what commercial spectacles and literature cannot be sold or distributed to you—if you choose to live in that community. The community sets up standards for itself, and has a right to legislate to protect those standards.

b) Nobody is imposing his morality on anybody. It is only the consensus of the community that determines the standards of public decency. When that consensus is properly manifested in public law, that is community or public morality, not "ours."

c) This implies there should be no law regulating the traffic in pornography.

10. Obscenity is a "victimless crime."

Answer:

a) There is no such thing as a "victimless" crime. In every crime there is a seller or seducer, and the person who purchases, or the seduced. That person is the immediate victim, and society is the ultimate victim, for with each seduction the moral fabric of society is diminished. The "victimless crimes" theory is an active and insidious attack on almost all laws dealing with public morality, maintaining there is "no victim" when "consenting adults" indulge in drugs, prostitution, obscenity, homosexuality, adultery, incest, gambling, etc.

b) A glaring instance of victimization in obscenity are the children used in child pornography.

c) For centuries civil communities have maintained laws against such behavior as detrimental to the public health, morals, and welfare.

d) Denmark and the Boston Combat Zone have recently and vividly proved that increase in commercial pornography causes concentration of violent prostitution and organized crime.

11. When "consenting adults" go to see a dirty movie, no one is being harmed.

Answer:

Regarding so-called "consenting adults," the United States Supreme Court said in *Paris Theatre* in 1973: "We categorically disapprove the theory that obscene films acquire constitutional immunity from state regulation simply because they are exhibited for consenting adults only. Rights and interests other than those of the advocates are involved. These include the interest of the public in the quality of life, the total community environment, the tone of commerce and, possibly, the public safety itself."

12. If you'd let pornography flow freely, people would get bored and the problem would take care of itself.

Answer:

This boredom or satiation theory is invalid. (See "Where Do You Draw the Line?" edited by Dr. Victor B. Cline). Heavy users of pornography do not get bored. They go deeper and deeper into more and more bizarre forms of it.

b) Professor Irving Kristol said in the same volume, "I would like to go along with this theory (boredom), but I cannot. I think it is false. The sexual pleasure one gets from pornography is autoerotic and infantile; put bluntly, it is a masturbatory exercise of the imagination when it is not masturbation pure and simple. Now, people who masturbate do not get tired of masturbation, just as sadists don't get bored with sadism and voyeurs don't get bored with voyeurism. In other words, infantile sexuality is not only a permanent temptation—it can easily become a self-reinforcing neurosis."

c) Denmark is often brought up when the boredom theory is espoused. Denmark legalized pornography, the argument goes, and porn profits dropped because people got bored.

Denmark's porn profits are falling, but not because of boredom. Underworld infiltration of the porn industry and gangland violence and tie-ins with traffic in narcotics forced Copenhagen police to close down dozens of smut dens, and all live sex shows have been outlawed. (Associated Press Reports, 1972-76)

d) Remember, every day children are seeing pornography for the first time. Pornography strikes at children in the mails, on newsstands, etc.

13. How do you define obscenity?

Answer:

How I define obscenity is not the issue. The Supreme Court has defined obscenity to the satisfaction of most. It said: the test for obscenity is: Materials which "taken as a whole appeal to the prurient interest in sex, which portray sexual conduct in a patently offensive way, and which, taken as a whole, do not have serious literary, artistic, political or scientific value."

14. But the Supreme Court left it to communities to decide what is obscene.

Answer:

This is an oversimplification and a misleading one. Community Standards is not *the* test for obscenity, but a *part* of the test for obscenity, and has been part of the test for obscenity since 1957. In 1973 the Court said: "The basic guidelines for the trier of the fact must be: a. whether 'the average person, applying contemporary community standards' would find that the work, taken as a whole, appeals to the prurient interest . . . b. Whether the work depicts or describes, in a patently offensive way, sexual conduct specifically defined by the applicable state law,'' etc. It is the ''trier of the fact,'' a jury or a judge, who decides what is obscene under the guidelines.

15. How is a producer or publisher to know his material is obscene when the Court can't even decide what is obscene?

Answer:
The Court has decided what is obscene, and it is up to a person who traffics in pornography to be alert to, and know what the Supreme Court decisions are. The Court said in its landmark *Miller* decision when it defined obscenity, ''We are satisfied that these prerequisites (the three-part test) will provide fair notice to a dealer in such materials that his public and commercial activities may bring prosecution.''

16. Why be concerned about obscenity when there is so much violent crime?

Answer:
They are related. Pornography outlets breed and attract violent crime.

17. The pornography industry is flourishing and growing. So the American people must want it or simply don't care.

Answer:
Certainly there are some who want it. That's what makes it so profitable. And obviously there are some who don't care. But all surveys show that the majority of Americans are vehemently opposed to the traffic in pornography and want it stopped. The majority *do* care; but they are confused and discouraged in the face of a highly organized industry and the loud prophets of false freedom. This is the reason why the organization, Morality in Media, exists; to expose the false prophets, to vindicate the true freedoms of responsibility under

law, and to raise in an organized way the voice of the majority who care very much about standards of public morality.

One of the major factors in the growth of the pornography traffic is the lack of vigorous enforcement of obscenity laws, particularly at the federal level.

18. Why bother enforcing the law? The "adult" book stores and porno movie houses keep operating while their owners are in the courts.

Answer:

Continuous, vigorous enforcement of the law is the answer. When arrests and prosecutions begin, the sex industry is put on warning. Prison sentences, fines, legal fees will put the pornographers out of business. Atlanta, Jacksonville, and Cincinnati are clean cities because of vigorous, continuous enforcement of the law. And experts say that with aggressive enforcement of federal law, the back of the porno industry would be broken in eighteen months.

Cableporn

1. If you don't want to see pornography on cable TV, turn the dial.

Answer:

I have no obligation to do this. The obligation is on the cable operator not to transmit pornography. The U.S. Supreme Court said in 1978 that the "turn the dial" argument does not hold water. I have already been assaulted. The Court said it's like running away after I have been punched by a mugger.

2. But I want to see porno programming in my home, and I pay to see it.

Answer:

You might pay for it, but once the cable operator transmits pornography through that wire, it is released on the community; it becomes the community's business; and the community can legislate against it. And the law is aimed, not at you, but at the cable operator who transmits the cableporn to you. You might also want to pay $5 to see a porno movie in a movie house, but it is against the law for the owner to exhibit it to you. You might want heroin in your home, and pay for it, but it is against the law for the seller to sell it to you.

3. The cable operator says only those who pay for cableporn will get it, so if you don't want it, you don't have to subscribe to it.

Answer:

Again, once the cableporn is released on the community, it is the community's business. In addition, there have been complaints from many areas of the country that the signals of cableporn channels are "bleeding" over onto the sets of people who don't subscribe to them. Audio signals are clear and unscrambled; video signals fade in and out clearly.

There is also cableporn on public access channels, which come into homes for the basic cable fee; and any child can tune in these channels at any time.

4. If you don't want your children to see cableporn, the cable operator is offering lock boxes.

Answer:

There is no lock box that is a match for a child's curiosity. Children in Michigan have already found a way to bring a cableporn channel into non-subscribing homes simply by jiggling the key on the cable channel selecter. In addition, it came out in a Utah case that one key opens up every lock box in the country.

5. In trying to get a law passed that prohibits cableporn, you're trying to tell me what I can see.

Answer:

Nobody can tell you what you can see. But the community can tell you what cannot be transmitted through the cable wires if it chooses to do so. The community sets up standards for itself, and has a right to legislate to protect those standards.

6. A law prohibiting cableporn would interfere with the First Amendment rights of the cable operator, with the free flow of information.

Answer:

There is already a federal law prohibiting the *broadcasting* of the obscene, indecent and profane, and it has never interfered with the free flow of information in broadcasting. Cablecasting, the U.S. Department of Justice has decided, does not come under the purview of the broadcasting law because it is transmitted through wires. There is almost no regulation on cable TV and there should be. There should be the same regulation of cable as there is of broadcasting. Different technology or not, it comes through the same instrument, the TV set, into the home.

7. If you don't want cableporn bleeding over onto your set, don't subscribe to cable at all.

Answer:

Nobody should have to deprive himself of cable TV because a few porno peddlers are giving the industry a bad name. Cable TV is a medium of magnificent potential, of infinite variety. We need a law.

8. What about "consenting adults" who want to see porn movies in their home?

Answer:

The U.S. Supreme Court said in *Paris Theatre* v. *Slaton*, "We categorically disapprove the theory . . . " See question 11 above.

Notes

Chapter One
The Social Crisis

1. "According to the California Department of Justice, the nation's pornographers do a good $4 billion-a-year business. . . . The estimate may be grossly conservative. 'Two or three times that is more like it,' says one West Cost police officer. . . . " "The X-Rated Economy," *Forbes* (Sept. 18, 1978), p. 81.

   Forbes reports that ten leading sexually oriented magazines generated $475 million in 1978; the 780 "adult" film theaters have 2 million admissions per week and grossed $365 million and that $100 million goes into "sexual toys."
2. Ernest Van Den Haag, "Pornography and Censorhip," 13 *Policy Review* (Summer 1980).
3. Stephen A. Kurkjian, Ed., et al, "Spotlight: the Pornography Industry," *Boston Globe* article I: "Pornography Industry Finds Big Profits in New Markets," February 13-18, 1983.
4. *People* v. *Mature Enterprises, Inc.* 343 N.Y.S. 2d 911 (1973).
5. Nick Cavnar, "The Victims of Victimless Crime," *New Covenant*, September 1981.
6. Neil Gallagher, *The Porn Plague* (Bethany House, 1981), p. 16ff.
7. Dr. Judianne Densen-Gerber, "What Pornographers Are Doing to Children: A Shocking Report," *Redbook Magazine*, August 1977, p. 86; Densen-Gerber, "Developing Federal and State Legislation to Combat the Exploitation of Children in the Production of Pornography," *Journal of Law and Medicine*, September 1977, with Stephen F. Hutchinson, Esq.
8. Norval Morris, "The Law Is a Busybody," *New York Times Magazine*, April 1, 1973; and Herbert Packer, *The Limits of the Criminal Sanction* (Stanford, 1968).

Chapter Two
What Pornography Is

1. "Symposium: Obscenity and the First Amendment," *Capitol University Law Review*. "Obscene Evils v. Obscene Truths: Some Notes on First Principles," p. 647.

A recent exception to the usual bland treatment of this issue by scholarly journals is: "Colloquium: Violent Pornography: Degradation of Women Versus Right of Free Speech," 8 *New York University Review of Law and Social Change* (1978-79), Number 2. These are articles by radical feminists who rightly see pornography as exploitation of women. (Hereafter referred to as "Colloquium.")

2. Still, most "family" newspapers today do print the ads for X-rated films, a fact that suggests their resistance to the spread of pornography is less than principled.

3. Reo M. Christienson, "The Judgment on *Hustler:* Sanity, Not Censorship," *The Cincinnati Enquirer*, Feb. 11, 1979.

4. These are Citizens for Decency Through Law, Morality in Media, and National Federation for Decency. Their addresses appear in the last chapter of this book.

5. Charles H. Keating, Jr., to Mr. James Manney of Servant Publications, October 12, 1983.

6. Harry Clor, "Obscenity and Freedom of Expression," *Censorship and Freedom of Expression: Essays on Obscenity and the Law*, Harry Clor, Ed. (1971) p. 97; also see Harry Clor, *Obscenity and Public Morality* (University of Chicago Press, 1969).

7. Sarah J. McCarthy, "Pornography, Rape, and the Cult of Macho," *The Humanist*, September/October 1980, p. 16.

8. In "Colloquium," p. 215.

9. "Current Reading," *The Public Interest* 112 (1971), quoting Black in the *Village Voice* (Nov. 26, 1970).

10. "Pornography Industry Finds Big Profits in New Markets," *The Boston Globe*, Feb. 13-18, 1983.

11. The U.S. Supreme Court later upheld the U.S. statute criminalizing this conduct as "promoting the sexual performance of a child," even though perhaps not technically obscene, since it is also child abuse (*People of New York* v. *Ira Paul Feber* [1982]).

12. Tom Gerety, "Pornography and Violence," 40 *University of Pittsburgh Law Review* 627, (1979), p. 628. This article contains a useful bibliography of literature on pornography and violence, pp. 652-660.

13. Charles H. Keating Jr., *Statement on Senate Bill 1722*, United States Senate Committee on the Judiciary (October 15, 1979), p. 7. The Bill was proposed for the purpose of recodifying the federal criminal laws.

This *Statement* is a very useful document. Mr. Keating, who was a member of the 1969-70 Presidential Commission on Obscenity and Pornography, may well be the nation's leading expert in this area; the *Statement* is an easy-to-read summary of the major facets of the pornography problem; it also contains Mr. Keating's dissenting *Report* to the Commission (originally published September 30, 1970), and a legal Memorandum analyzing S.1722 along with amendments strengthening it. The *Statement* should be available from Citizens for Decency Through Law, 2331 W. Royal Palm Rd.—#105, Phoenix, AZ 85021.

Chapter Three
Pornography and Behavior

1. Lester A. Sobel, Ed., *Pornography, Obscenity and the Law*, pp. 37-38. Facts on File, 119 W. 57th St., New York 10019.
2. Victor B. Cline, Ed., *Where Do You Draw the Line? An Exploration into Media Violence, Pornography, and Censorship*, (Brigham Young University Press, 1974), p. 205.
3. James Q. Wilson, "Violence, Pornography and Social Science," *The Public Interest*, No. 22 (Winter 1971), reprinted in Ray C. Rist, Ed., *The Pornography Controversy* (Transaction Books, 1975), p. 225; Cline, "Another View: Pornography Effects, the State of the Art," and "The Pornography Commission: A Case Study of Social Scientists and Social Policy Decision Making," in *Where Draw Line*, Cline, ed., pp. 203 and 245; Harry Clor, "Commentary on the Report of the Commission on Obscenity and Pornography," *Where Draw Line*, Cline, ed., p. 335; Herbert L. Packer, "The Pornography Caper," *Commentary*, Vol. 51, No. 2, (February 1971).
4. "Porno Books 'Responsible' for Attacks," Ft. Wayne, Indiana, *Journal Gazette*, Sept. 22, 1973.
5. *Presnell* v. *State*. 243 S.E. 2d 496 (1978).
6. Charles H. Keating, Jr., Letter dated August 11, 1969, reprinted as Exhibit C in Mr. Keating's dissenting *Report*, Commission on Obscenity and Pornography (September 30, 1970).
7. Paul C. Vitz, *Psychology As Religion: The Cult of Self-Worship* (William B. Eerdmans Co., paper ed., 1982), pp. 40-41.
8. For discussion of the difference between true art and obscenity see: Harry M. Clor, *Obscenity and Public Morality* (University of Chicago Press, 1969), pp. 211-271; Walter Berns, "Pornography versus Democracy," *The Public Interest*, No. 22 (Winter 1971), pp. 3-24; W.A. Stanmeyer, "Obscene Evils v. Obscure Truths," 7 *Capitol University Law Review* 647, at fn 28, p. 663, citing Howard, "On Evil in Art," *Christianity Today*, Dec. 17, 1971, pp. 4-5.
9. Berns, "Pornography Versus Democracy," pp. 11-12.
10. Clor, *Obscenity and Morality*, p. 163.
11. Michael Levin, a professor of philosophy at City College of New York, wrote in June, 1982 issue of *Commentary*:

> When parents object to profanity in school books, they are invariably met with the answering cries of "censorship" or "thought control," and warned of the dangers of tampering with the First Amendment. Yet . . . one of the most extensive thought control campaigns in American educational history has gone completely ignored. I am referring to the transformation, in the name of "sex fairness," of textbooks and curricula at all educational levels, with the aim of convincing children that boys and girls are the same.

Indeed, a dismantling of "sex roles" has virtually superseded transmission of information as the aim of the classroom. (Franky Schaeffer, *A Time For Anger: The Myth of Neutrality* [Crossway Books, 1982] pp. 142-43).

12. *Paris Adult Theatre I* v. *Slaton*, 413 U.S. 49 (1973).

Chapter Four
Pornography and Crime

1. "The Big Business of Selling Smut," *Parade* Sunday Supplement (August 19, 1979).

   During the last decade, many large urban newspapers have exposed the connections between organized crime and the production and promotion of pornography. A comprehensive list would be unduly long; but a sampling follows: "Mob's Role Is Target in Fight against Porno," *The Miami Herald* (March 25, 1974); "Police Link 'Porn' to Crime Syndicate," *Christian Science Monitor* (July 8, 1977); "Mafia Controls Distribution of Smut Books," *Cleveland Plain Dealer* (October 13, 1975); "Mob Here Reaps Child Porn Cash," *Chicago Daily News* (May 17, 1977); "Diary of Slain Smut Peddlar," *The Charlotte News* (June 12, 1978); "FBI Raids Operation Run by Porn King Here," *Cleveland Press* (Feb. 14, 1980); "St. Louis Pornography Firm Linked with Mafia," *St. Louis Post-Dispatch* (July 3, 1977); "Denver Pornography $3 Million Scene—Ties to Organized Crime," *Denver Post* (August 21, 1977); "Pornography: The Real Story—A Portrait of the Mob's Man," *The Washington Star* (February 15, 1978); "Who's Who in Smut Shows Mob Influence," *Indianapolis Star* (December 30, 1977); "Porno Trade in Capital Tied to Mob," *Staten Island Advance* (May 22, 1978); "Tie N.Y. Mob to Porn Here," *The Chicago Tribune* (July 7, 1977); "Mobsters Skim New York City Sex Industry Profits," *The New York Times* (July 27, 1977); and—finally—a federal government effort to enforce the law against all this: "55 Persons Indicted in Piracy of Films and in Pornography," *The New York Times* (February 15, 1980).

2. Richard A. Serrano and Richard D. Ralles, "Porn a Risky Business," *Kansas City* (Missouri) *Times* (September 9, 1978).

3. Wendell Rawls, Jr., "55 Persons Indicted in Piracy of Films and in Pornography," *The New York Times* (February 15, 1980), p. 1.

4. *Organized Crime.* "Report of the Task Force on Organized Crime of the National Advisory Committee on Criminal Justice Standards and Goals" (1976), quoted in: Lester A. Sobel, ed., *Pornography, Obscenity & the Law* (New York: Facts on File, 1979) pp. 29-30.

5. Ibid., p. 31.

6. "An Investigation of Racketeer Infiltration into the Sex-Oriented Materials Industry in New York City" (State of New York, Commission of Investigation, 270 Broadway, New York, N.Y. 10007), pp. 195-244.

7. Ibid., p. 204.
8. Ibid., p. 228-29.
9. See, e.g., Norval Morris, "The Law is a Busybody," *New York Times Magazine* (April 1, 1973); Eugene Doleschal, "Victimless Crime," *Crime and Delinquency Literature* (June, 1971); Edwin Kiester, Jr., *Crimes With No Victims* (The Alliance for a Safer New York, 1972); Herbert Packer, *The Limits of the Criminal Sanction* (Stanford, 1968). All of these writers, along with the very liberal American Bar Association "Individual Rights and Liberties" Committee, assert that pornography "has no victims" and thus should not be illegal.

   In this book I attempt to show the copious evidence proving that pornography has *countless* victims and should be controlled. Others who I believe have much the better of the argument agree; see, e.g., Walter Berns, *Freedom, Virtue and the First Amendment* (Louisiana University Press, 1957); Harry M. Clor, *Obscenity and Public Morality* (University of Chicago Press, 1969). See also my essay, " 'Victimless Crimes' and Public Morality," *Modern Age* (Fall, 1974), 369.
10. Herbert Packer, *Limits of Criminal Sanction*, p. 278-279.
11. Ibid., p. 279.
12. Ibid., p. 280.
13. Available from the Department of City Planning, City of Los Angeles, Room 561, City Hall, Los Angeles, California 90012; City Plan Case No. 26475, Council File No. 74-4521-5.3.
14. Ibid., p. 7. Emphasis in original.
15. Ibid., pp. 20, 51-55.
16. Ibid., p. 52.
17. Ibid., p. 31.

Chapter Five
Psychological Health

1. Frederic Wertham, M.D., "Medicine and Mayhem," *MD* Magazine (June 1978) pp. 11-13. Dr. Wertham is consulting psychiatrist at Queens Hospital Center, New York City. He was formerly associate in psychiatry, Johns Hopkins Medical School and Fellow of National Research Council, Washington, D.C. Dr. Wertham has done research on violence for many years and has written several books on the subject: *Dark Legend: A Study in Murder; Seduction of the Innocent; The Circle of Guilt; The Show of Violence; A Sign for Cain: An Exploration of Human Violence.*
2. Melvin Anchell, M.D., "A Psychiatrist Looks at Pornography," reprint of newspaper article based on Anchell, "Pornography Is Not the Harmless Recreation It Is Said to Be," *Liberty* (July/August 1977), p. 11; see also Anchell, *Sex and Sanity* (Macmillan, 1971); Anchell, *Sex and Insanity* (Portland, Ore.: Halcyon House, ed. Research Assoc., 1983).
3. Ernest Van Den Haag, "Pornography and Censorship," 13 *Policy*

Review 73, Summer 1980, pp. 77-78.

4. Ibid., pp. 79-80.
5. A point urged by a defender of pornography, Susan Sontag. Van Den Haag, "Pornography and Censorship," p. 78.
6. Anchell, p. 12.
7. Donnerstein, "Aggressive Erotica and Violence against Women," 39 *Journal of Personality and Social Psychology,* (1980) pp. 269-277. This article contains a useful bibliography of references to other publications on the same theme.
8. S. Feshbach and N. Malamuth, "Sex and Aggressions, Proving the Link," *Psychology Today*, November 1978, p. 111.
9. Dr. Victor B. Cline, address, "Aggression Against Women: The Facilitating Effects of Media Violence and Erotica," (Delivered April 8, 1983, University of Utah), reprinted in *NFD Journal*, October, 1983, pp. 14-18. This publication, which deals with sex and violence in the media, is available from National Federation for Decency, P.O. 2440, Tupelo, Mississippi, 38803.
10. Ibid., pp. 16-17.
11. Marjorie Smith, "Violent Pornography and the Women's Movement," 4 *Civil Liberties Review* 50 (1978).
12. Susan Brownmiller, "Pornography and the First Amendment" in *Colloquium: Violent Pornography*, p. 255. In her book, *Against Our Will: Men, Women and Rape*, (New York, 1975), Ms. Brownmiller rightly stated: "Hard-core pornography is not a celebration of sexual freedom; it is a cynical exploitation of female sexual activity through the device of making all such activity, and consequently all females, 'dirty.'" . . . (Quoted in J. H. Court, "Rape and Pornography in Los Angeles," for Australian Psychological Society Annual Conference [August, 1977], p. 8.d). D.E. Russell urges: "The point about the relationship between pornography and rape is this: pornography even at its most banal, objectifies women's bodies. Women become things . . . Men are reared to view females in this way, pornography thrives off this, and feeds it, and rape is one of the consequences." (D. E. H. Russell, in "Pornography: A Feminist Perspective" [San Francisco, Symposium Paper, 1977]).
13. David Holbrook, "Pornography and Hate," *Family Review* (Second Quarter 1981), p. 3-5. Available from A.L.L., P.O. Box 490, Stafford, Virginia 22554.
14. Joseph Sobran, "Nothing to Look At: Perversity and Public Amusement," *The Human Life Review* 80, p. 83.

Chapter Six
Exploitation of Women

1. None of this is surprising. Men have chemical and glandular drives different from women's; physiologically, as opposed to psychologically, these are usually more powerful or at least express themselves

more forcefully. Men tend to react more quickly, physiologically to visual stimulus.

2. "Porn," *The Student Lawyer*, December, 1980, p. 26.
3. Frederic Wertham, "Seduction of the Innocent," (1954) 9]-91, cited in Harry Clor, *Obscenity and Public Morality* (University of Chicago Press, 1969), pp. 163-64.
4. Liebart, Davidson, and Neale, "Aggression in Childhood: The Impact of Television," reprinted in Victor B. Cline, Ed., *Where Do You Draw The Line?* (Brigham Young University Press, 1974), p. 120.
5. Marjorie M. Smith, " 'Violent Pornography' and the Women's Movement," 4 *The Civil Liberties Review* 50 (January/February 1978).
6. Andrea Dworkin, "Pornography: The New Terrorism," in: "Colloquium," p. 215.
7. Ibid., pp. 219-223.
8. Ibid., p. 189.
9. Andrea Dworkin, "Pornography's Part in Sexual Violence," *Los Angeles Times*, May 26, 1981.
10. Linda T. Sanford and Mary E. Donovan, "What Women Should Know About Pornography," *Family Circle*, February 24, 1981, p. 12.
11. Malamuth and Feshback, "Sex and Aggression: Proving the Link," *Psychology Today*, Nov. 1978, p. 111; Malamuth, Feshback and Jaffe, "Sexual Arousal and Aggression: Recent Experiments and Theoretical Issues," *Journal of Social Issues* No. 2 (1977), p. 110; both are cited in the Gerety Bibliography, p. 659. (See note 2, chapter 2.)
12. Teresa Hommel, "Images of Women in Pornography and Media," in "Colloquium," pp. 207-214; examples on pp. 109-210.
13. Ernest Van Den Haag, "The Case Against Pornography," *1980 Policy Review*, The Heritage Foundation, Washington, D.C., reprinted in *The Chicago Tribune* March 20, 1980.

Chapter Seven
Exploitation of Children

1. Quoted in Sam Janus, Ph.D., *The Death of Innocence: How Our Children Are Endangered by the New Sexual Freedom* (William Morrow and Co., 1981), p. 210.
2. "Children for Sale: Pornography's Dark New World," *Ladies Home Journal*, April 1983, reprinted in *Reader's Digest*, July 1983, p. 52.
3. John G. Hubbell, "Father Ritter's Covenant," *Reader's Digest*, October 1980, p. 2.
4. Nick Cavnar, "Moral Outrage Isn't Enough," *New Covenant* September, 1981. Comparable episodes appear in articles by Rooney and Hubble, *supra ns* 2 and 3.
5. Recounted in the Covenant House *Newsletter* (September 1983); address: 460 West 41st Street, New York, NY 10036; phone (212) 613-0300.
6. *Presnell* v. *State*, 243 S.E. 2d 496 (1978).

7. See historical summary in: Comment, "Preying on Playgrounds: The Sexploitation of Children in Pornography and Prostitution," 5 *Pepperdine Law Review* 809 (1978) pp. 810-814.

8. Clifford L. Linedecker, *Children in Chains*, (New York: Everest House, 1981). Despite its grim subject matter, this superb book deserves the careful attention of every parent, judge, and law-enforcement officer who cares about our children.

9. Ann Burgess, et al., article 3, *Journal of Crime and Justice* 65, 68 (1980). The quotes appeared in the pre-publication manuscript, then titled "Syndicated Child Pornography." See also Burgess, *Child Pornography and Sex Rings* (Lexington, Mass: Lexington Books, 1984); See R. Lloyd, "For Money or Love: Boy Prostitution In America" (1977); Sneed, et al., Series of investigative articles appearing in *Chicago Tribune*, May 15-18, 1977; "Kiddie Porn," *60 Minutes* transcript of CBS Telecast (May 15, 1977); Burgess, et al., "Child Sex Initiation Rings," 51 *American Journal of Orthopsychiatry* 110 (1973).

10. The record of Congressional hearings leading to the enactment of the Protection of Children Against Sexual Exploitation Act of 1977 (18 U.S.C. 2251-2253, Supp. III 1979) is replete with testimony concerning the manipulation and coercion of the young to produce "kiddie porn." See "Protection of Children Against Sexual Exploitation," the hearings before the Subcommittee to Investigate Juvenile Delinquency, Senate Committee on the Judiciary, 95th Congress, 1st session (1977); and "Sexual Exploitation of Children," Hearings before the House Subcommittee on Education and Labor, 95th Congress, 1st session (1977).

   The House hearings, for example, contain testimony from Lloyd Martin, Los Angeles Police Department, about the lease, then the sale, of a nine-year-old boy by his parents to an older man for sexual molestation. Other testimony identified child pornography actors as "throwaways. . . . who are neglected and abused"; as children "as young as six years old"; and as children of a parent "so [economically] desperate that he knowingly and willingly permits the child to be so abused." Joseph Freitas, San Francisco District Attorney, said that "I could continue to present case after case, a veritable litany of woes to support what has been claimed: that large numbers of American children are being coerced into performing sexual acts for pornographers."

11. Melvin Anchell, M.D., *Sex and Insanity* (Portland, Ore.: Halcyon House, 1983), p. 88.

12. Linedecker, *Children in Chains*, pp. 106-123.

13. Dr. Ann W. Burgess, Principal investigator, Research on the Use of Children in Pornography, Department of Health and Human Services, Office of Human Development (Debriefing on Child Pornography Projects, December 8, 1982), p. 5. Monograph available from Dr. Burgess, Department of Health and Hospitals, Peabody 3, 818 Harrison Ave., Boston, Mass. 02118.

14. *Preying on Playgrounds*, p. 819, n. 70, quoting New York

psychoanalyst Herbert Freudenberger.

15. Ibid., pp. 819-820, ns. 71-72: "Senate Committee on the Judiciary report on S. 1585, Protection of Children Against Sexual Exploitation Act of 1977, S. Rep No. 95-438, 95th Cong. 1st Sess. 6 (1977); see also Report to the Attorney General on Child Pornography in California (June 24, 1977), p. 18, which stated, inter alia, that on a single page of a certain California "underground newspaper," no less than 34 ads for sexual materials appeared, of which 18 offered child pornography and 9 of those 18 offered materials depicting bestiality (p. 5). See general authorities commenting on the harmful effect of disseminating pornographic materials to children: Dibble, "Obscenity: A State Quarantine to Protect Children," 39 *Southern California Law Review* 345 (1966); Wall, "Obscenity and Youth: the Problem and a Possible Solution," 1 *Criminal Law Bulletin*, 8, 21 (1965); "Note," 55 California Law Review 926, 934, (1967); "Comment," 34 *Ford Law Review* 692, 694 (1966); Green, "Obscenity, Censorship and Juvenile Delinquence," 14, U. *Toronto Law Review* 229, 249 (1962); Lockhart and McClure, "Literature, the Law of Obscenity, and the Constitution," 38 *Minnesota Law Review* 295, 373-385 (1954); Note, 52 *Kentucky Law Journal* 429, 447 (1964). Especially see Dr. Gaylin of the Columbia University Psychoanalytic Clinic, reporting on the views of some psychiatrists in "Galin, The Prickly Problem of Pornography," 77 *Yale Law Journal* pp. 579, 592-93 (1968) where he states:

> It is in the period of growth [youth] when these patterns of behavior are laid down, when environmental stimuli of all sorts must be integrated into a workable sense of self, when sensuality is being defined and fears elaborated, when pleasure confronts security and impulse encounters control—it is in this period, undramatically and with time, that legalized pornography may conceivably be damaging.

16. Rhoda L. Lorand, Ph.D., "A Psychoanalytic View of the Sex Education Controversy," *Journal of the New York State School Nurse Teachers Association*, vol. 2 (fall 1970), pp. 13, 24. Available from NYSSNTA, 23 Point View Dr., East Greenbush, NY 12061.

17. Melvin Anchell, M.D., "So What's Wrong with the Cave Man?" (privately published booklet, 1971), p. 7. See also Janus, *The Death of Innocence*, p. 233, concluding his chapter on "Child Sex Exploitation":

> In my own experience, children who have premature relations with adults, whether they are forced or not, often suffer a prolonged trauma, which manifests itself in disturbed sleep and appetite, persistent nightmares, trouble at school. It seeems unquestionable still that . . . sexual relations of any sort between children and adults are *always* an unwarranted interference with the normal process of growth and can only hurt the child." (Emphasis in original)

18. The other states: Arizona, Colorado, Delaware, Hawaii, Kentucky, Louisiana, Maine, Massachusetts, Michigan, Mississippi, Montana, New Jersey, Oklahoma, Pennsylvania, Rhode Island, South Dakota, Texas, West Virginia, Wisconsin. List taken from Petition for Writ of Certiora for State of New York, FN 2, pp. 8-9, (U.S. Supreme Court October Term, 1981).

   Since child pornography is particularly an urban problem, it is surprising that the New York Attorney General's Brief did not include such heavily urbanized states as Illinois, Ohio, and California. The U.S. Supreme Court, in a footnote, stated there is a large number of states with such statutes.

   In any event, having the laws on the books is only the first step: *enforcement* is also essential.

19. 52 NY 2d 674, 439 N.Y.S. 2d 863 (1981).

20. *New York* v. *Ferber* 458 U.S. 102 S. Ct. 3348 (1982).

21. For an excellent summary of the history of *Ferber* and of New York's efforts, see: Elaine Jackson Stack, "Preventing the Sexual Exploitation of Children: The New York Experience," 56 *New York State Bar Journal* 11, February, 1984.

22. There is some response from social-service agencies. Linedecker lists (Appendix II, p. 319) 212 "Runaway Youth Programs," spread among all 50 states and the District of Columbia. This list, based on a Directory published by the U.S. Office of Juvenile Justice and Delinquency Prevention, L.E.A.A., U.S. Department of Justice does not include such good programs as Odyssey House and Covenant House in New York, or Boys Hope Program in St. Louis and other cities.

Chapter Eight
Pornography and the Law

1. Patrick Devlin, *The Enforcement of Morals* (1961).

2. See: Herbert Packer, *The Limits of the Criminal Sanction* (Stanford, 1968); Norval Morris, "The Law Is a Busybody," *New York Times Magazine*, April 1, 1973; Eugene Doleschal, "Victimless Crime," *Crime and Delinquency Literature* (June 1971); David Brudnoy, "Decriminalizing Crimes Without Victims: The Time Is Now," *New Guard* (April 1973), p. 4.

3. Lester A. Sobel, Ed., *Pornography, Obscenity and the Law* (Facts on File, 119 West 57th St., New York 10019; 1979), p. 7.

4. For a concise explanation of the "educative" role of law, see the author's " 'Victimless Crimes' and Public Morality," *Modern Age* (Fall 1974), pp. 369-379.

5. *Rosen* v. *U.S.*, 161 U.S. 29 (1896). The constitutionality of the statute was not challenged; rather, the main issue was the omission of the obscene materials from the indictment: the lower court thought it improper to put obscene materials on court records. For a capsule history of obscenity law in the last century, see Franklyn S. Haiman,

ed., *Freedom of Speech*, (National Textbook Company, Skokie, Illinois, with the ACLU, 1976), pp. 112-114.

6. *Butler* v. *Michigan*, 352 U.S. 380 (1957), º383.
7. *Roth* v. *U.S.*, *Alberts* v. *California*, 354 U.S. 476 (1957).
8. *Memoirs* v. *Massachusetts*, 383 U.S. 413 (1966), a plurality, not majority, opinion. At no time did more than three Justices adhere to the "utterly without redeeming social value" test.
9. An excellent analysis of the difference between "art and trash" appears in: Henry D. Clor, *Obscenity and Public Morality: Censorship in Liberal Society* (University of Chicago Press, 1969), pp. 210-245.
10. Leonard W. Levy, *Freedom of Speech and Press in Early American History* (Harper, 1963), deals with the Zenger case *passim*.
11. But some perceptive writers have begun to urge the insight that pornography is not "speech" at all; see, e.g., Frederick Schauer, "Speech and 'Speech'—Obscenity and 'Obscenity': An Exercise in the Interpretation of Constitutional Language," 67 *Georgetown Law Journal* 899 (1979). Schauer argues that "the prototypical pornographic item on closer analysis shares more of the characteristics of sexual activity than of the communicative process. The pornographic item is in a real sense a sexual surrogate."
12. A good summary of Supreme Court views on obscenity in the 1960s appears in: *Lane* v. *Sunderland*, *Obscenity: The Court, the Congress, and the President's Commission* (American Enterprise Institute, 1974), pp. 47-69.
13. *Redrup* v. *New York*, 386 U.S. 767 (1967).
14. *Ginsberg* v. *New York*, 390 U.S. 629 (1968).
15. *U.S.* v. *Reidel*, 402 U.S. 351 (1971).
16. *Miller* v. *California*, 413 U.S. 15 (1973).
17. *Paris Adult Theatre I* v. *Slaton*, 413 U.S. 49 (1973).
18. The Recommendations appear at pp. 51-64 of the *Report of the Commission on Obscenity and Pornography*, (Washington, D.C.: U.S. Government Printing Office, 1970), and in many commentaries; see, e.g., Ray C. Rist, ed., *The Pornography Controversy* (Transaction Books, 1975), p. 64-84; and Victor B. Cline, *Where Do You Draw the Line?* (Brigham Young University Press, 1974), pp. 185-202. See also Sunderland, pp. 71ff.
19. James Q. Wilson, *Violence, Pornography, and Social Science*, in Rist, pp. 225-243; Sunderland, pp. 75-84; see also the Hill-Link Minority Report, cited, with approval by Chief Justice Burger, in *Miller*; and the extensive dissenting Report by Commissioner Charles H. Keating, Jr., available from Citizens for Decency Through Law.
20. See: Complaint for declaratory judgment, U.S. District Court for the District of Columbia [Civil Action No. 2671-70] filed on September 9, 1970, and Order of Court and stipulation of dismissal, September 14, 1970.
21. On May 21, 1984, Congress passed the Child Protection Act of 1984, Public Law 98-292, amending chapter 110 (relating to sexual exploitation of children) of Title 18 of the U.S. Code. This law is a step in

the right direction, if vigorously enforced. At the ceremony to sign the Bill, President Reagan also announced plans to create a Commission, later called a Task Force, in the Justice Department to review what has happened to society because of pornography, since the controversial Obscenity and Pornography Commission of 1969-70. If knowledgeable and realistic persons are appointed to this Commission, and if its Executive Director pursues the evidence of the real-world connection between pornography and sex crimes, the Commission can do much good. But if the Commission should be composed of persons chosen on criteria unrelated to their demonstrated expertise and track record in favor of public morality, it, like its predecessor, may well do more harm than good.

Chapter Nine
What You Can Do

1. See articles and books by clinical psychologists, e.g.: Ernest Van Den Haag, "Pornography and Censorship," 13 Policy Review 73 (Summer 1980); Sam Janus, Ph.D., *The Death of Innocence* (New York: William Morrow, 1981); Melvin Anchell, M.D., *Sex and Insanity* (Portland, Ore.: Halcyon House, 1983).
2. Michael McManus, "Virginia man enthusiastic in his war against pornography," *The Ann Arbor News*, March 24, 1984.

Index